THE INNER LIVES OF MARKETS

THE INNER LIVES
of MARKETS

HOW PEOPLE SHAPE THEM—
and THEY SHAPE US

RAY FISMAN *and* **TIM SULLIVAN**

PUBLICAFFAIRS
NEW YORK

Book Design by Jack Lenzo

Library of Congress Cataloging-in-Publication Data
Names: Fisman, Raymond, author. | Sullivan, Tim, 1970– author.
Title: The inner lives of markets : how people shape them—and they shape us
  / Ray Fisman and Tim Sullivan.
Description: First edition. | New York : PublicAffairs, [2016] | Includes
  bibliographical references and index.
Identifiers: LCCN 2016001296 (print) | LCCN 2016006755 (ebook) | ISBN
  9781610394925 (hardback) | ISBN 9781610394932 (ebook)
Subjects: LCSH: Economics. | Free enterprise. | Markets. | Consumer behavior.
  | BISAC: BUSINESS & ECONOMICS / Economics / Microeconomics. | BUSINESS &
  ECONOMICS / Purchasing & Buying. | BUSINESS & ECONOMICS / Consumer
  Behavior.
Classification: LCC HB171 .F545 2016 (print) | LCC HB171 (ebook) | DDC
  381—dc23
LC record available at http://lccn.loc.gov/2016001296

First Edition
10 9 8 7 6 5 4 3 2 1

To my priceless children—RF

To Wendy—TS

CONTENTS

PREFACE

This book started about ten years ago with a trip to The Coop bookstore at the Massachusetts Institute of Technology. On a shelf in the science section was a book that contained reprints of the most important physics papers of the twentieth century, together with an explanation of what they accomplished and why they were important. The book included, for instance, Einstein's work from 1905, his annus mirabilis, when he published four papers that changed how physicists (and eventually the rest of us) thought about time, space, mass, and energy. It also included papers that led to innovations like the first atomic bomb—science that had a direct impact, quite literally (sorry), on the world.

This was important stuff, but the source material was often impenetrable to nonscientists—certainly too technical for the likes of us. But even for scientists, *why* a particular idea was so revolutionary can often be lost because few scientists study the history of their field. The idea, though familiar, loses its historical and social context. So each article in the book was accompanied by a lucid, engaging essay explaining the innovation in lay person's terms, and placing the idea in context. Otherwise, most of the papers would have remained so much indecipherable mathematics to all but a trained physicist.

It was, we thought, an interesting approach to the history of science, told through both scientific importance and social change, written for people who had more than a passing interest in physics but who lacked the expertise to parse the original source material.[1]

Being economics nerds (one of us is a real economist, one of us just pretends), we thought it might be fun to do the same thing with economics. To that end, we informally surveyed a bunch of economists to find out which academic economics papers they thought were the most important within the rough boundaries of World War II on the one end and, say, the early 2000s on the other, reasoning that it would be hard to judge the long-term historical importance of ideas published any later than that.

When we looked at that list of papers and thought about what we could do with the information, it occurred to us that these relatively esoteric academic papers had had, like their counterparts in physics, an outsized influence. That seemed worth exploring, not by reprinting the original papers but by examining how those ideas have lived in the world.

This half-century's worth of economic thought—often as incomprehensible to outsiders in its original formulations as Einstein's investigations into the theory of Brownian motion is to non-physicists—has been used to make markets work better and, in an ever-widening set of applications, has helped them reach more deeply into our lives. *The Inner Lives of Markets* explores the intersection of those economic ideas and our lives.

THE INNER LIVES OF MARKETS

INTRODUCTION
TERMS OF SERVICE

At 109 Lincoln Street in Rutland, Vermont, stands a dilapidated yellow clapboard building. Rutland was incorporated in the late nineteenth century, flush with money from the marble quarries just outside town. But the past few decades haven't been kind to the city, notable these days as much for its opioid epidemic (the subject of several *New York Times* stories), as for the nearby mountains, which still draw leaf peepers in the fall and skiers in the winter.

To one side of 109 Lincoln is an empty parking lot. Across the street stands the former Lincoln Elementary School, which now houses Rutland Area Christian School, private and interdenominational, serving pre-K through grade twelve.

In many ways, Rutland is classic small-town America, and the yellow clapboard building is emblematic of that life. It was, once upon a time, Percy P. Woods, a neighborhood grocery store. Percy himself was an enterprising young man, born around 1886, just as the city was taking off. He started on his road to entrepreneurial glory in the 1920s, selling maple syrup by mail order and using the money he made to open Percy P.'s (as it was known) as a dry-goods store, updated by the next owner into a small local grocer. Around 1970, Bob Dow, a former traveling tombstone salesman, and his wife, Edna, bought the store. Bob became a whiz at the butcher counter, and Edna took over business operations in the tiny upstairs office. She also cooked a widely renowned roast beef and made subs in the deli. They lived within walking distance of the store, in the house on Adams Street where Edna had grown up.

Lincoln Elementary, the school across the street, served the families in the surrounding neighborhoods, kindergarten through grade six. That also meant that moms (and it was mostly moms in those days) who picked up their kids could swing by Percy P.'s (as it was still called) and grab a missing dinner ingredient or some detergent. They'd also get an avuncular greeting from Bob and have their order checked out by Dot, the cheery cashier. And if they needed a babysitter, they could check to see if Bob and Edna's daughter might be available.

Percy P.'s was subject to the laws of supply and demand that define every market, no matter how big or small. Bob and Edna balanced the books in their upstairs office. They thought about how it would affect sales if they marked up the price of Tide and carefully calculated how many boxes of detergent they'd need to meet their customers' monthly demand. They decided what to put on sale and used markers—the king-size permanent ones (that smelled so distinctively toxic they aren't made anymore)—to make the signs that called customers' attention to the lower prices. Some customers bought on credit, which they'd pay at the end of the month, but not everyone was afforded this privilege. Edna kept track of who had too big a tab or had passed a bad check and politely but firmly demanded that they pay in cash. Bob was nice and polite, too, but he kept an eye on the front door, all the more so when the end-of-school bell rang next door, sending a gang of preteens into the store. (And yes, they tracked inventory "shrinkage" resulting from the pilfered candy and soda that walked out of the store despite Bob's efforts.)

From Percy P.'s to Today

Of course, now, when you're running out of detergent, you can hit an Amazon Dash Button that's connected to your Wi-Fi and more will arrive on your doorstep in a couple of days (or, depending on where you live and what you're willing to pay, even a couple of hours). Or get a ride to a great restaurant with Uber or order a meal from Sprig. Busy parents can hire a sitter or nanny using Care.com. Don't want to go out to the movies? Netflix and chill. And ever fewer kids still walk to their neighborhood schools.

We've experienced some radical changes—changes that have taken us far beyond the world of Percy P.'s. The way the story is often told, we've gotten from there to here because of technological innovation—internet marketplaces replacing Main Street and the mall, Uber and Airbnb disrupting the taxi and hotel industries. But there's more to this story than techno-determinism.

As important as technology is, it's only one of the driving forces behind the changes we've witnessed. We're here to tell you about a parallel set of innovations and insights that have also played a central role: ideas that started in the academic study of economics over the past half century and have had an outsized effect on how scarce goods are allocated—how, that is, we get the stuff that we want. This is the economic architecture that underlies what appears to be merely a shift in technology.

Sometimes, the change has been so radical that you might not even realize you're observing a market in action because it's so far removed from the standard price system that we've come to equate with market exchange. But economists no longer limit themselves to money and pricing in thinking about how the wants and desires of individuals determine how resources (whether kidney beans, kidneys, or kids in a kindergarten class) are distributed. The very definition of what constitutes a market has changed.

New forms of transacting are popping up not just on iTunes, Google, Uber, and e-commerce sites (although algorithms driven by economic theory of recent vintage lie under the hood of these websites). Economists have also changed the way we think about—among other things—how to match medical residents to hospitals or donor kidneys to dialysis patients, how governments sell broadband spectrum, and how donations are distributed among food banks across America.

Economic Theory and You

We wanted to tell the story of the sometimes complicated interactions that have landed us where we are today—surrounded by market interactions that have not only replaced grocery stores like Percy P.'s but also schools like Lincoln Elementary. Our goal is to clarify the relationship between the markets we interact with every day, innovations in economic theory over the past fifty years or so, and how the world has changed because of it. *The Inner Lives of Markets* weaves together those three strands, aiming to understand how economic theories have illuminated the real world and how those theories have in turn helped shape the way the world works.

Beyond that, we also explore the consequences of more—and more sophisticated—markets slowly creeping into ever more areas of our everyday lives. We're now immersed in markets built on these theories, and that has an effect on how we interact and which goals we prioritize.

To telegraph where we'll end up: markets have changed things for the better—overwhelmingly so. But progress doesn't come without costs. Not least, we're entirely uncertain about where all of this change will take us. We're in the midst of a grand social experiment that has elevated efficiency above all other virtues. Even the experts can't know where we're going, even when they claim they do (maybe especially so then). To even have a conversation about this experiment in increasing marketization in the name of ever-increasing efficiency, we all need a deeper understanding of the ideas that are driving it.

Lots of conversations about "free markets" descend into shouting, finger pointing, and acrimony. They feature, on the one side, those who fear all market innovations as crypto-libertarian plots to deregulate the world and enslave us all and, on the other, market fundamentalists who see free and open markets as the solution to all the world's ills—and then some. But we have to understand the fundamental issues that are in play to have that conversation. We have to agree on the facts, which is what this book is about.

Order of Operation

We begin in an unlikely place—a German POW camp during World War II. The experiences described by one young British prisoner convey just what makes free markets so attractive. The spontaneous creation of a market at Stalag VII-A ensured that scarce resources were allocated efficiently. When everyday items—food, toothpaste, cigarettes—are in scant supply, the market's efficiency doesn't just make life more comfortable; it's a matter of survival.

That story of the Stalag's market is prologue to the story of how economists' understanding of markets changed from the postwar years to the present. Economics has become intensely mathematical, which, for a while, was perhaps a diversion. But the economists that came of age in the late 1950s and '60s directed their efforts—while retaining the discipline's precision in reasoning—toward confronting questions and puzzles in many corners of the real economy: how markets can fall apart completely if sellers know more about what they're selling than buyers do, and how participants might be able to salvage these markets through such diverse means as attending colleges that don't teach you anything useful, dropping cars off cliffs during Super Bowl ads, or getting face tattoos (yes, you read that right).

In their efforts to understand the real world, economists provided the analytical underpinnings and ideas that then began to shape the world itself. The field of auction design, which has shaken up the millennia-old practice of selling items to the highest bidder, was launched, with thirty pages of algebra, in the *Journal of Finance* in 1961. Recent work on two-sided markets like Uber or Google that sit between customers and drivers or between web searchers and advertisers has helped to guide the strategies of companies looking to build the next killer platform. We now even have market designers who have shifted from describing markets to shaping them to a desired image in an effort to address a particular problem, whether assigning students to the right schools or matching medical residents to hospitals.

This isn't an intellectual history of economics since World War II, nor are we aiming to be comprehensive in our coverage. Instead, we hope that our selective history of recent market insights and design can get us to a place where we can better confront our complicated and often fraught relationship with markets. Rather than react viscerally to them, we can be better informed on when markets actually work their magic—where, as we'll see near the end of the book, they've have made the world far, far better despite some initial resistance. Maybe, then, we can start a conversation on how we feel about the increasing intrusion of markets into our lives. For as we'll see, their influence doesn't end when we click at checkout—markets may be changing who we are.

The World's Terms of Service

We've been pretty blithe about how we navigate this new world, often failing to even recognize the extent to which new markets have come to surround us. There's a good reason for that: the pace of change, accelerated by technology, has been astonishingly fast, leaving us scarcely a moment's pause to take a breath. To make better choices on what kinds of markets and how much of them we want in our lives, we had better first understand the ideas behind them. As we'll see, not even the market designers themselves have all the answers: economics is an inexact science, and every time we participate in a market innovation—each time we hail a ride via a smart phone or download a song from iTunes—we're part of a massive social experiment whose ultimate consequences are unknown.

It's a little like how we handle those "terms of service" agreements when we download new software. We simply click the "I have read and agree" option. No you haven't. No one has. What we need is a simplified terms of service that spells out exactly what we're agreeing to so we can make sensible choices. That's what *The Inner Lives of Markets* aims to do for the market-driven existence that we find ourselves living: it's a simplified "terms of service" for the world we live in now.

1

WHY PEOPLE LOVE MARKETS

R. A. RADFORD'S STIFF UPPER LIP AND
THE ECONOMIC ORGANIZATION
OF POW CAMPS

In 1939, R. A. Radford left his studies in the Cambridge University economics department to join the British Royal Army. He was captured in Libya in 1942 and transported to a transitional prisoner-of-war camp in Italy before being sent to Stalag VII-A, a POW camp just outside the town of Moosburg, thirty-five miles northeast of Munich. The Germans had built the camp to hold ten thousand Polish prisoners from their 1939 offensive, but when Radford arrived, it was overflowing with soldiers of many nationalities, from Americans to Yugoslavs.

Radford made it through the war and headed back to Cambridge to complete his degree. He used his experience in Stalag VII-A as the basis of his first and, from what we can tell, last published academic article, which appeared in the November 1945 edition of the economics journal *Economica*.

The world that Radford describes in "The Economic Organisation of a P.O.W. Camp" isn't what you might expect. It's a description of the Stalag VII-A as a market, one marked by thriving trade and value creation in the absence of labor: the Red Cross delivered care packages filled with tinned milk, tinned carrots, jam, butter, biscuits, "bully beef" (also known as corned beef), chocolate, sugar, treacle, and cigarettes. But of course not every prisoner liked biscuits and beef equally, so they started trading. A bit of butter plus two cigarettes for your tinned milk. Several rations of coffee for a fresh tea bag.[1]

At first, this system of exchange arose out of goodwill. But underlying much of it was a cold, rational calculus of camp residents looking to survive with a just a little more comfort in the camp's harsh conditions. And "comfort" meant different things to different prisoners—a cup of coffee to some, a cup of tea to others.

Because the Germans cordoned off each country's soldiers—the camp's equivalent of trade barriers—only a privileged few could interact with prisoners from other nations. Those who could made the most of it, becoming expert traders. The French really liked coffee, so the handful of British troops who could enter the import-export business with them first traded for Red Cross coffee rations with their fellow Brits (who only wanted tea and sold their coffee cheap) and then turned around and sold it at a significant premium to the French (in exchange for the tea the French didn't want but the British did). Soldiers from both nations were better off as a result, even after British traders took their cut. Even the coffee-loving French had their price and traded much of the British-acquired coffee extract to guards who in turn sold it on the black market to cafés in town, where decent coffee was even scarcer than inside the camp.

Similarly, the Gurkhas from the Indian contingent didn't eat beef—and many didn't speak English. So the lucky men who could communicate with them would trade tinned carrots, which were otherwise near worthless, directly for beef, which traded well among the Europeans.

These individual preferences and motivations reproduced a miniature global economy within the camp's walls.

Soon enough, the inmates realized the need for a system of exchange that went beyond Stone Age barter. Lacking hard currency, they denominated the price of everything not in pounds or in dollars but in cigarettes.[2] A ration of margarine might be bought for seven cigarettes, the equivalent, for instance, of one and a half chocolate bars, and so on. For the most part, prices were well known and consistent among the camp's many huts that acted as local markets. And when prices did get out of line—say, six cigarettes for a margarine ration in one hut and eight in another—astute and energetic arbitrageurs quickly profited by buying low and selling high, erasing the price differential in the process.

As with any economy, Stalag VII-A's was unstable. Deliveries of cigarettes by the Red Cross sparked immediate inflation, doubling virtually overnight the cigarette-denominated price for having a pair of trousers washed and pressed. As POWs smoked their cigarettes, prices once again fell. And when the Red Cross's supply of cigarettes was interrupted altogether, the camp economy suffered intense deflation. When the men started breaking down machine-made cigarettes and rolling their own, faith in the now-debased currency disappeared.

The market wasn't a libertarian free-for-all. Senior officers felt that unfettered markets needed a little oversight and intervention. Following the advent of cigarettes as money, the ranking British officer set up a shop where goods could be traded at no profit, based on generally accepted prices listed on wooden boards around the camp, taking much of the guesswork and uncertainty out of buying and selling. Because of concerns over health—some were even worried that heavy smokers would risk starvation and infection by trading away all of their food and hygiene supplies for smokes—Red Cross toilet articles were excluded from trade.

By 1945, three years after Radford's arrival, Moosburg's population had swelled with new POWs. It held, by some estimates, around 110,000 Poles, Brits, Americans, Greeks, Yugoslavs, French, Belgians, Dutch, and Indians. As the camp became more and more crowded, conditions grew dire. Frank Murphy, an American navigator of a B-17 bomber that was shot down during a raid on Münster, arrived at Moosburg after a four-hundred-mile forced march in February 1945, just as the war was nearing its end. In his account, Murphy doesn't mention any signs of a market.[3]

Instead, Murphy described the Stalag like this: "Our cheerless barbed wire encircled world was comprised exclusively of austere, dilapidated buildings, grungy tents, mud, and clusters of gaunt, emaciated men in shoddy, worn out clothing occupying every inch of unused space they could find." Their diet included black bread made from sawdust, turnips, and a soup known as "green death." The sanitary conditions were "unspeakable." The lucky ones slept in bunks, while most bedded down on tables or on the bare ground.

Stalag VII-A had become so packed and unruly, with new POWs unfamiliar with the market's prices and protocols and deliveries from the Red Cross so inconsistent, that the camp economy had largely fallen apart amid the uncertainty, chaos, and extreme scarcity.

But then, blessed relief: "On 12th April, with the arrival of elements of the 30th U.S. Infantry Division," Radford wrote, "the ushering in of an age of plenty demonstrated the hypothesis that with infinite means economic organization and activity would be redundant, as every want could be satisfied without effort." In other words, if everyone can get everything they want, you don't really need markets, which probably doesn't describe the situation most of us are in.

After completing his degree, Radford immigrated to the United States, where he worked at the International Monetary Fund (and wrote what sounds like the most boring IMF staff paper ever: "Canada's Capital Inflows: 1946–1953"), rising to the position of assistant director of the Fiscal Affairs Department at his retirement in 1980. He passed away in 2006. Presumably, he or his wife did some grocery shopping in the Washington, DC, area markets. But he didn't write about it.

$$$

Markets don't just make life more comfortable in the odd POW camp. They can save lives.

Consider the contrast between the experiences of Radford and his fellow prisoners in Germany, who were free to run their markets, and those in the Pacific, whose captors outlawed trade. In Japanese camps, captured senior officers doled out food and other supplies, and violators of the no-trade rule were punished with solitary confinement, which served as a de facto death sentence. Death rates were twelve times higher at the hierarchical camps of the South Pacific compared to the laissez faire (economically speaking) camps in Germany.

To state the obvious, there were many differences between German and Japanese camps than merely the freedom to trade. Consider the infamous Sandakan camp of Borneo, infamous in large part because of the aptly named death marches to relocate prisoners to a camp at Ranau that took place under its commandant, Captain Hoshijima Susumu. There, the death rate among nonescapees was 100 percent. There is no market system that would have saved its unfortunate residents. (For a grim illustration of the conditions under the Japanese, watch the movie *Unbroken*, based on the book of the same name: it is unflinching in its representation of the horrors of Japanese prison camps.)

So overall, it's not surprising that the Japanese camps had a higher mortality rate than the German ones. Figuring out exactly what role freer markets might have played in the differing mortality levels in the different camps requires a more sophisticated approach. It comes to us from Clifford Holderness, a serious World War II buff who also teaches finance at Boston College. Some years ago, he was browsing the National Archives' World War II Prisoners of War Data File, which had just been released online. The economist in him naturally wondered how the largely unexplored trove of data could be put to good use. Together with his colleague, Jeffrey Pontiff, he set out to examine what led to better outcomes in POW camps.

Under the brutal treatment of some Japanese captors, just surviving to liberation was an achievement. So Holderness and Pontiff examined whether survival rates could be predicted by the degree of hierarchy that existed in a given camp. The extent to which the chain of command remained intact among units entering the camp was, they argued, a good predictor of whether command and control (rather than markets) would prevail in the camp economy.[4]

Holderness and Pontiff don't compare survival rates at German camps to Japanese ones—the differences are too multifaceted and complex. Rather, they analyze whether, among German camps and among Japanese ones, more hierarchy leads to greater or lesser survival.

Just as Sandakan's POWs had the random misfortune to be assigned to a camp run by a sadist like Susumu, some prisoners ended up in camps with varying degrees of hierarchy based on the ranks of the Allied soldiers that happened to be captured nearby. Some might have a full chain of command from general to colonel to major down to the lowliest privates. Others might be more dominated by rank-and-file soldiers. If hierarchy helps a community survive, those with a healthy portion of officers should do better.

But that's not what Holderness and Pontiff found: their analysis puts them firmly in Radford's camp, so to speak, showing that markets did save lives, or at least typical military hierarchy led to far worse outcomes.

As the officer composition of a camp more closely matched the military's established hierarchy, survival declined.[5] This wasn't because officers sacrificed their men to increase their own chances of survival. Despite privileges afforded to officers by their captors, death rates were highest among the POW officer corps. It also didn't seem to be the result of strong social networks among groups of low-ranked POWs that arrived at camps together. Survival rates at hierarchical camps were worse even for strangers who arrived solo, or in very small groups, like downed air force pilots and crew.

This led the authors to favor an interpretation that trading served prisoners better than rule by officers (even self-sacrificing ones who gave their lives to ensure their men could survive).

They also found personal accounts of POWs to support the view that fostering markets was a life-and-death matter in many camps. Lester Tenney, interned by the Japanese, explained how trading helped prisoners reallocate food rations in case of illness. A sick prisoner might not be able to keep his rice ration down and couldn't save it amid the camp's filth, heat, and humidity. So instead of leaving a day's allotment to rot or risk vomiting it into a pit, trade allowed a current ration to be swapped for a future one. Even with the risk of beating or death, POWs still felt that, given the benefits, trading increased their chances of survival. Said Tenney: "I was willing to gamble my life to trade for food."

The Japanese caught Tenney trading on a grand scale, by camp standards. They sentenced him along with his fellow traders to be beheaded. In his memoirs he recalls saving himself and others in the docket by telling the camp commander, "Men, don't try to fool the Japanese; they are very smart. Do what they say and you will live to see your families again. Do what I did, and you will die here in Japan." The commander, his "chest puffed out to its fullest . . . impressed us all as being one very happy man." Tenney and the rest were sent to the guardhouse with clean water and a full meal each day for ten days. Whoever said flattery will get you nowhere?

Tenney survived the camps, as well as the Bataan Death March, and went on to apply his trading instincts as a finance professor at Arizona State University.

$$$

Broadly speaking, a market is just a technology, a mechanism where participants have the chance to directly affect resource allocation through an expression of their preferences—a way for deciding how goods are distributed based on which ones people want and how badly they want them.

Often enough, that "expression of preferences"—just how much you want something—means the price you're willing to pay. Some inmates in Stalag VII-A, especially those who could trade with the German guards, valued coffee, which commanded a high price in the currency of cigarettes because it was much in demand. You give a grocery store money for peanut butter. Traders exchange promissory notes for pork bellies in a pit at a Chicago commodities market. You buy and hold stocks for your retirement fund and check their value (occasionally or obsessively) on the finance page. The prices that emerge in these marketplaces as a result of all this trading does a remarkable job of capturing the availability of all of these goods and services, relative to our wants and desires. As Austrian economist Friedrich Hayek put it, "Prices are an instrument of communication and guidance which embody more information than we directly have." In a way, market prices know us better than we collectively know ourselves.

If that's all markets were, you might think this exercise is rather pointless: a market is a market is a market, after all. How much could possibly have changed?

True enough. We all still exchange money for goods and services. And yet the leaps we've experienced over the past half century have been profound. We've witnessed expansions in the scale and scope of markets—the result of the migration of many transactions online. Amazon is called "The Everything Store" for a reason. And the same computing revolution that has enabled the internet has also made many transactions (though by no means all of them) millions of times faster and cheaper. In many of its new shapes and incarnations—the innumerable e-commerce sites, the airline ticket you bought online for your next vacation, the digital magazine subscription that substitutes for the paper ones you used to read—today's markets are governed by the same market principles that Radford documented in 1945, just a lot bigger and faster.

At the same time, these principles are getting applied in ever-broader, more novel, and more sophisticated contexts. Ever wonder where the ads come from when you perform a Google search? They appear based on principles of auction design that didn't exist in 1945. And that smart phone in your pocket? It's both a technological and market innovation, what economists call a multisided platform. You acquire apps—sometimes paying for them but not always—created by developers on the other side of the trade. The free apps survive by delivering messages from advertisers who sit on yet another side of the phone-as-platform. And finally the phone itself is essentially another piece of the phone "ecosystem" built around the operating system—Android or iOS or Windows—that ultimately directs traffic in this many-sided set of relationships.

There are increasing numbers of markets where prices don't play any role at all. When a dater logs onto Match.com and chooses to contact some eligible bachelors and not others, it's an expression of preference in the market for love. Yet there are no prices, and no money changes hands.

Our era has become defined by the deliberateness with which we've designed mechanisms with the aim of streamlining how just about everything imaginable is allocated or exchanged. At the root of these changes is a revolution in our understanding of markets that has paralleled the market innovations we observe taking place around us. Some of economists' new ideas have produced completely new market institutions—like the auctions that govern Google's AdWords algorithm and the allocation of kidneys to transplant recipients or students to schools. Other insights have improved our understanding of how old-fashioned markets work, enabling us to design and manage them that much better.

These twin revolutions of market insights and market practice have often intersected. The field of economics has shifted from merely describing the world—first in words, then in mathematical equations—to profoundly shaping how the world works.

The theories might not have had such outsized influence— theories don't act on their own, after all—were it not for the infiltration of commerce by academically trained economists.[6] That this incursion has taken place during the much-hyped Age of Big Data has afforded economists ever more capacity to track behavior, tweak and refine their models, and ideally on each iteration make the market function a little bit better.[7]

We don't normally think of economists and their mathematical models as social engineers, mad scientists using the world as their laboratory. They measure, predict, describe. But over the past fifty years, economists have slowly gone from developing theory to designing how we buy the goods we want and interact with one another. So this book is also the story of those whom markets have enchanted, and the journey that markets have taken since World War II, as they've been studied, refined, obsessed over, harnessed, modified, designed, and released into the real world to wreak what they may.

On the whole, we think, this is a good thing. These newly designed markets were created to cut through inefficiencies— to reduce gaps in what buyers and sellers know, to make use of underutilized assets like idle cars and empty apartments, to get rid of pointless haggling over prices, and, overall, to do a better job of helping participants on each side of the market find one another. And thank God for that because, all else equal, when it comes to efficiency, more is often better.

Yet markets hardly provide the unalloyed benefits that their champions might have you believe. The world is not simply a question of markets versus command-and-control in POW camps. Markets are not the solution to every social problem. This is more easily discerned when you realize that in this would-be paradise of efficiency, all is not necessarily equal. As the virtue of efficiency, quietly and without much notice, becomes an end rather than a means, other values that we as a society aim to uphold get the cold shoulder. Democracy wasn't designed to be as smooth, as fast, as profitable, or as efficient as possible.[8]

There's yet another dimension to the story. The wider effects of the increasing intrusion of markets in our lives are entirely unclear, and we have no idea what society might look like at the end of it all. Guided by the insights and intuitions gleaned from the recent revolution in economic thought, policy makers and companies have been conducting what amounts to a grand experiment with new kinds of markets that, as we'll see, sometimes have unforeseen or unintended consequences.

Practically speaking, we're living in the middle of this experiment, the principles of which were created in the pages of esoteric journals by economists, in the labs of high-tech companies, often (but not always) overlaid by a particular political orientation that comes with being starstruck by the efficiency of the market.

Although the experimental subjects (that's us) are nearly always blind to the consequences of this experimentation, don't suffer under the delusion that market planners have all the answers. Science doesn't provide clear guidance on any of this stuff. People (including at least some economists) have a delusional sense about what economic science is capable of forecasting. We need more than a superficial consideration of what new market mechanisms mean for the vast majority of people and whether the type of world that market revolutionaries aspire to is one we'd want to live in.

We're all complicit. Every time you book a room on Airbnb, order a car through Uber, browse on Amazon, or click on an ad—so convenient! so easy!—you help the process of reshaping our social institutions, possibly into something that none of us would recognize. You may not mean to, but you do.

The question for someone in the midst of an experiment is, Do you want to be an experimental subject?

Maybe.

But to really know the answer, you have to have a better sense of the possible consequences, both personally and socially. And because the scientists have some hypotheses but don't—can't, really—know the outcome, we're left with competing visions of the world. At one end of the spectrum are the back-to-the-earthers who want us all to stay local and barter for what we need. At the other end are market fundamentalists who want to shred the very fabric of society and resew it according to the specifications of unfettered free markets.

Market fundamentalists come in many shades and gradations, but the ones we hear from most often tend to be the most lacking in nuance. They preach the power of free markets—without ever appearing to consider any trade-offs, which is a little ironic, given that understanding trade-offs is at the center of economic analysis. Their arguments would be easy to dismiss but for two facts. First, many of them wield a surprising amount of power in the real world, in particular in politics or business (more than a few of those railing against big government can be found cozily holed up preaching cyberutopia in Silicon Valley). And why not? There's something appealing about a clear story with a practical trajectory to solve the world's ills, which is what the markets-as-salvation narrative provides.

The market fundamentalists have another thing going for them: sometimes, they're right—just ask a focus group of former POWs of camps in Germany and Japan. Markets are powerful tools for making sure that, all things considered, people end up with whatever they most value.

To know where you fall on the spectrum, you have to understand the new markets that are shaping our world. And we have to make choices about the trade-offs. That's the grand ambition of this book: to help you understand the choices you face a little bit better so that we can make some fundamentally important decisions about the role markets will play in our future.

To be able to make those choices and understand the new world that we're living in, it's useful to begin by exploring the enormous revolution that economics—the discipline most responsible for the reshaping of our world—was going through right around the time that R. A. Radford returned to England to begin his career as an economist.

2

THE SCIENTIFIC ASPIRATIONS OF ECONOMISTS, AND WHY THEY MATTER

HOW ECONOMICS CAME TO RULE THE WORLD

By the time Radford penned his essay on the economy of Stalag VII-A, he was building on a tradition that was centuries old. But something dramatic was happening right around the same time. Economics was becoming mathematical. Math provided economists with the tools they needed to strip away extraneous details that obscured fundamental truths about how the world worked: it allowed them to cut to the heart of the matter. In turn, that spare mathematical approach allowed economists to suggest how the world might work much better and gave new generations of businesspeople the tools to build muscular businesses on the bones of theory. That shift to math allowed economics, eventually, to take over the world.

If you find yourself wondering why we're reviewing this history of economic thought, it's not because we think you should know esoteric economic theory from the mid-twentieth century. It's because the men and ideas we discuss paved the way for economics to have an outsized influence on our lives. That's not some kind of condemnation. It's a fact. Before the mathematization of economics, the discipline was often confused and contradictory, and economists could hide weak logic behind dazzling prose. When economists were forced to lay out their assumptions and steps in an argument in spare, precise terms, this was no longer possible: all was laid bare.

In the early years of the math revolution in economics, the eventual connection to and influence on the real world may have been hard to find amid the dense notation and algebra. But without laying this foundation, we'd argue, economics would never have become so powerful as a way to interpret the world and as a means to shape it. Abstracting from the specifics of any particular situation allowed economists to create general models, which in turn empowered them to make general predictions and, in the words of sociologist Kieran Healy, to ultimately "dispense advice on everything from childrearing to global climate change."[1]

That's not to say that the classical and neoclassical economists didn't use math. They did. Karl Marx's thousands of pages of passionate argumentation included extended technical discussions that, as economic historian Robert Heilbroner put it, are argued "to a point of mathematical exhaustion." His contemporary, the Frenchman Léon Walras, identified economics as, fundamentally, a mathematical discipline, and Vilfredo Pareto, an Italian engineer and sometime economist, used his mathematical background to further the discipline as well.

But, as Gérard Debreu, a Nobel Prize–winning economist and president of the American Economics Association, wrote in 1991, it was only with the closing of World War II that "economic theory entered a phase of intensive mathematization that profoundly transformed [the] profession."[2] In 1940, less than 3 percent of the refereed pages of the thirtieth volume of the *American Economic Review* "ventured to include rudimentary mathematical expressions." By 1990, that percentage was up to over 40 percent.

Marion Fourcade, a sociologist at the University of California at Berkeley, analyzed the economics profession and confirmed Debreu's back-of-the-envelope musings. It wasn't until just after World War II that mathematics became almost the sole focus on the discipline. "For much of the post–World War II period," Fourcade writes, "flexing one's mathematical and statistical muscles and stripping down one's argument to a formal and parsimonious set of equations was indeed the main path to establishing scientific purity in economics."[3]

s$$s

Radford, writing after the war, found himself in deep conversation with the classical economists of the nineteenth and earlier centuries—even as the profession was on the cusp of its mathematical transformation. Radford's larger message about the efficiency of markets was, after all, one of the main points of Adam Smith's metaphor of the invisible hand, an idea that first appeared in Book IV of his epic *Wealth of Nations* in 1776.

To Smith, the power of the market was clear, requiring no formal proof of its veracity or elucidation of the precise circumstances where it would be truer than others. Smith largely asserted that individuals can pursue their own self-interest and make society as a whole better off.[4] It was a revelation.

Generations of economists that followed—collectively referred to by economic historian Heilbroner as "the worldly philosophers"—extended Smith's ideas. These early economists aimed to tackle big questions about how the economy worked (and whether it could be made to work better), weighing in on such important matters as market function (and dysfunction), the origin of value, business cycles, and unemployment. It was set in motion by Smith and carried on for one hundred years thereafter by the classical economists—David Ricardo, Thomas Malthus, Karl Marx, Vilfredo Pareto, among others. It was continued for nearly one hundred years more by neoclassical economists like Thorstein Veblen, John Maynard Keynes, and an enduring hero of free-market proponents, Joseph Schumpeter.

Pareto, who lived from 1848 until 1923, is emblematic of both the worldliness and precision of these towering figures in the history of economic thought. He was well experienced in matters of business but also well schooled in the language of math that was already deployed to describe economics and commerce. In writing about the significance of Pareto's work in *Econometrica* in 1938, Roman economist Luigi Amoroso notes that Pareto had earned a doctorate in engineering from the Polytechnic Institute of Turin in 1869, at the age of twenty-one, and practiced as a manager for twenty years (rising to be president of the Italian Iron Works) before turning to economics. He then made the unusual transition to professor at the University of Lausanne, where he taught for the next two decades.

Among Pareto's enduring contributions were his incisive observations on the distribution of income. Building from his calculation that the richest 20 percent of Italians owned 80 percent of the country's land, Pareto posited that incomes in an economy tend to be distributed according to a "power law." (Power law distributions will often generate extreme inequality, making Pareto an unlikely hero of the Occupy movement.)

Most memorably, though, he used his mathematical skills to extend Smith's invisible hand arguments, introducing a particular criterion by which economists could assess social well-being.[5] This welfare principle, named Pareto efficiency by British economist I. M. D. Little, suggests that we may judge an economic system by whether it's possible, through some series of trades or exchanges, to make at least one individual better off without making anyone worse off. This is a fairly minimalist view on social welfare—for example, if a tax policy brought millions of people out of poverty but in the process left Donald Trump with ten fewer dollars in his bank account, it would fail to be a Pareto improvement because someone—even someone as rich and odious as Trump—is made worse off. But that also means that Pareto improvements should be changes that *everyone* can agree on because, by definition, everyone is better off.

It is exactly this type of work that served as a bridge between Smith's stories and the mathematical economists of the twentieth century who took Pareto's work and showed, rigorously, that efficient markets are Pareto optimal (i.e., no two market participants can improve their lot through further exchange, once the economy is up and running).[6] The worldly philosophers created a set of conjectures and principles. Their mathematical descendants gave these ideas precision, which allowed them to glean further insights and predictions from their models.

Radford—with his mathless assessment of Stalag VII-A's market—was engaged more in an economics that was soon (perhaps sadly) to become a thing of the past.

His story about the value created by markets was intimately linked to the long-running debate among nineteenth-century economists (and still going on during Radford's grad school days) on where value comes from. This back and forth helped link Radford's essay to, among other things, Karl Marx's obsessive pursuit of a labor theory of value.

In the 2,500 pages that constitute *Das Kapital*, Marx (a worldly philosopher whose mathematical work hasn't exactly stood the test of time) spells out in excruciating detail that for any item price equals value equals labor. That is, the "real" price of everything can be expressed in the total amount of labor required to produce it. This labor theory of value had limited meaning in the camp, where labor was itself banned by the Geneva Convention, so value came not from work but from the fact that different people wanted different things.

Radford could readily observe that, for him and his fellow inmates, value came from the market. In his own way, Radford was using his experiences in the POW camp to respond to Marx's theories and to those who still advanced those ideas in the Cambridge economics department.[7] It's a very nineteenth-century dialogue, and one that Marx would have easily followed.

This debate, while now firmly settled in the economics community, continues today among producers everywhere. It's a distinction that every would-be seller on Etsy, the marketplace for handmade goods, would do well to keep in mind. Few people care that it took you three days to knit that ugly scarf; it's still ugly and no one wants it. It doesn't matter if the yarn is really expensive (since making it required someone *else* to do the work of hiking to the Andes to procure the fleece, which had to be washed, carded and combed, spun, and set). If no one likes the scarf, it's not really worth anything to anyone except perhaps your mother.

Radford didn't just share a common set of questions with the classical and neoclassical economists. He, as did they, used observation and logical reasoning based on a set of well-established principles, together with clear exposition. He was among the last of his breed. Soon, math would come to dominate the field.[8]

$$$$

It's not as if economists, one day after the end of World War II, sat down in their ivory tower to decide that powerful mathematical techniques held all the answers. It was a process that happened over time. First, economic problems lent themselves to analysis by math. If each person, as in Smith's description, "intends only his own gain," you can think of them as maximizing their happiness (what economists call utility). There's a well-established machinery in mathematics for working through maximization problems—calculus—which could crystalize the choices faced by society's consumers and producers in a set of algebraic expressions.

These mathematical descriptions of the world could look a lot like the equations that physicists created to describe objects in motion. Economics has never achieved the same level of rigorous modeling as physics, but such precision was, for a long time, an aspiration for the discipline. If only economists could write models as precise as James Clerk Maxwell's 1865 description of the electromagnetic field—in only eight equations!

Maxwell's success—really, the successes of mathematically based physics more generally—showed how one could use math to, in Debreu's words, "study systems of forbidding complexity." It's turned out that the interactions among a collection of individuals that comprise an economy are more unpredictable than the interactions among a set of particles that constitute matter. But perhaps enough of the essence of markets could be distilled into algebraic form.

This approach had many benefits: math created a common language that pushed for weaker assumptions, stronger conclusions, and greater generality. And it allowed economists, as a group, to start creating a concise, logical system that described the world, much the way physicists have done. (Critics of this approach had emerged already at the beginning of the twentieth century. The eminent Austrian American economist Joseph Schumpeter described Pareto's theories as "arid generalizations" that did little to move the field forward.[9])

Mathematical models were easily assessed for logical errors. (At least superficially so: there was always the question of what assumptions one chose to make to shrink the market down to a few pages' worth of algebra.) Errors were apparent right there in the math, not hidden behind wordplay or unspoken assumptions. The math was also, in its own way, simple and clear.[10]

That clarity and simplicity allowed for a rigor that stands in sharp contrast to the standards of reasoning that were accepted even in the late 1930s. As Debreu wrote, "Few of the articles published then by *Econometrica* or by the *Review of Economic Studies* [two high-end economics journals] would pass the acid test of removing all their economics interpretations and letting their mathematical infrastructure stand on its own." Economists, at least at the time, mostly regarded this mathematical revolution as a step forward.

Outside influences also shaped the discipline and pushed it in an increasingly mathematical direction. One, the Cowles Commission for Research in Economics, founded in Colorado Springs in 1932 by businessman and economist Alfred Cowles, aimed to link economic theory more closely to math and statistics in an effort to model the economy. Cowles was inspired by the Great Depression and driven by the desire to bring scientific rigor to the study of the economy. The foundation's founding motto was "Science is Measurement."[11]

The second, the RAND Corporation, first established as a joint project by the Douglas Aircraft Company and the US Department of War in 1945, used game theory to analyze the United States's geopolitical position relative to the Soviet Union. Game theory—a mathematical approach to analyzing strategic choices—emerged from the work of Princeton mathematician John von Neumann in the 1930s, who collaborated with his economist colleague Oskar Morgenstern to write *Theory of Games and Economic Behavior* (published in 1944), which launched the field. Their book provided an analytical framework for figuring out, say, what Pepsi should do if Coke lowers its prices. That depends on how Pepsi's CEO thinks Coke will respond, which in turn depends on what Coke's CEO expects that Pepsi's response to their price reduction will be. And so on. Game theory was a way of cutting through the infinite regression of "what he thinks I think he thinks . . ."

Although technical, some of von Neumann and Morgenstern's ideas eventually filtered into the mainstream, and so resonated with the public imagination that the two researchers found themselves on the front page of the *New York Times* in 1946 under the headline, "Mathematical Theory of Poker Is Applied to Business Problems."[12] Game theory, though, was about much more than just business. Most famously, perhaps, RAND economists and mathematicians developed the doctrine of nuclear deterrence by mutually assured destruction (MAD) under the guidance of then defense secretary Robert McNamara (himself an economist by training).

Von Neumann and Morgenstern's *Theory of Games and Economic Behavior* is, in concentrated form, the story of how the new mathematical science of economics could operate and change the way the world works in arenas small (poker) and earth shattering (thermonuclear war). Von Neumann is alleged to have fine-tuned his mathematical models of strategic interaction based on the poker games he played with American generals during the Manhattan Project. Playing cards with great military minds turned out to be useful to Morgenstern in appreciating the critical aspects that govern different sorts of interactions. He later wrote, when discussing the difference between "games" of Cold War strategies and chess (a popular analogy), "The cold war is sometimes compared to a giant chess game between the United States and the Soviet Union, and Russia's frequent successes are sometimes attributed to the national preoccupation with chess. The analogy, however, is quite false, for while chess is a formidable game of almost unbelievable complexity, it lacks salient features of the political and military struggles with which it is compared."

Chess allows for no bluffing. Both players have full information on the rules of the game and the current state of play. Not so in poker—or the game of global thermonuclear war. Those who consistently win at poker "rely on their ability to perceive opportunities offered by each changing situation, and on artful deception through bluffing." Morgenstern concluded that if "chess is the Russian national pastime and poker is ours, we ought to be more skillful than they in applying its precepts."[13]

This overlap between some quite esoteric mathematical game theory and the real world reflects the overall argument of *The Inner Lives of Markets*: von Neumann and Morgenstern took something instinctual and messy and provided a clear path forward using logical and coherent math. Arcane mathematical, economic reasoning found fertile ground in real-world interactions like poker and mutually assured destruction. Their *Theory of Games* gave precision to the way we think about strategy—and also the way we strategize.

But this begs the question of why right-leaning RAND and left-leaning Cowles each turned to math. One reason it was seen as useful at both organizations is that, unlike words, mathematical theorizing presented what seemed a coldly objective analysis, devoid of political considerations. (The modern equivalent are think tanks on both sides of the political aisle that make claims of objectivity on the premise that they "let the data speak.") This was perfect for both analyzing the Cold War with the Soviets as a strategic game—a major focus of RAND—and making the field of economics safe for mathematically inclined immigrants and others who might otherwise have been in danger of being seen as left-leaning Communist sympathizers, many of whom ended up at Cowles.[14]

Combined, these developments led to the rapid construction of a body of economic theory that was powerful, insightful, clear, and seemingly objective. This work described in precise mathematical terms the conditions that defined competitive markets, and predicted—again, with precision—the market transactions that would ensue.

If it didn't look quite like any market you'd encounter in practice, a glimpse of every market that ever was could be found in the math: the upside of abstraction was generalizability and, one hoped, a universal set of insights about markets. This was the goal of this first wave of economic modelers: abstract yet clear generalizability.

Economists had thus moved from describing the real world to aiming to capture the essence of markets, and for the most part, what they saw was good. The men who follow in the rest of this chapter were some of the main protagonists in the early days of this history, but by no means the only ones. To tell the complete story would require a book of its own. What we're after is, instead, the broader path that economics took to become a pristine, mathematical discipline.

"Let Me Write the Textbooks"

Economics' postwar trajectory is captured, in a sense, by following the career of Paul Samuelson, one of the preeminent economists of the twentieth century. He's credited with not only helping economics develop a common language but also exposing this new language to the wider world. His economics textbook sold over four million copies during its decades-long reign as the bible for introductory economics courses worldwide.

Samuelson, a prodigy who entered the University of Chicago at the age of sixteen during the height of the Great Depression, received his PhD in economics from Harvard in 1941. A year *earlier*, MIT appointed him an assistant professor in its nascent economics department. He remained at MIT for the rest of his career, retiring in 1985, but remaining active until his death in 2009.

Samuelson won a Nobel Prize in economics in 1970. The Nobel committee singled out for praise his PhD thesis, which Samuelson had modestly titled "Foundations of Economic Analysis" (later published as a book). According to his biography on the Nobel Prize website, these new foundations were Samuelson's reaction to being "confronted by contradictions, overlaps, and fallacies in the classical language of economics."[15] In *Foundations*, Samuelson famously wrote that economists had been practicing "mental gymnastics of a particularly depraved type" and were like "highly trained athletes who never ran a race." It was a sound reprimand from a graduate student to the rest of the profession—his Harvard professors included—who lacked a logical coherence to their convoluted thinking, and whose work was utterly disconnected from the very real economic problems confronting America in the 1930s. His thesis was the beginning of his lifelong project to bring "unification—and clarification—in mathematics" to the profession.

Nobel prize winners are generally associated with a particular theory, insight or cohesive set of insights, or even a single specific paper. For Samuelson, rewriting economics in the new language of math was the contribution itself, often borrowing ideas already developed by physicists and mathematicians. He introduced, for example, the idea of Brownian motion (which he borrowed from physics) as a way of understanding financial markets, and a version of Henry-Louis Le Chatelier's principle (developed by chemists in the nineteenth century) as a tool for understanding market equilibrium. Samuelson didn't undertake this project alone but was responsible for many of its central contributions.

We also see in Samuelson the sense that the discipline imposed by mathematics made economics no less relevant to understanding real-world problems. His textbook served as a bridge between economic models and their counterparts in reality, shaping the views of generations of college freshmen. As he famously quipped, "I don't care who writes a nation's laws—or crafts its advanced treaties—if I can write its textbooks."[16]

Many see Samuelson's success as a testament to his genius. Sylvia Nasar, writing in the *New York Times*, said, "His reputation as the most brilliant theorist of his generation was secure by the time he was 30." His *Times* obituary calls him the "foremost academic economist of the 20th century."[17]

This is undoubtedly the case. But it's also true that the time was ripe for a mathematical revolution in economics. If it hadn't been Samuelson, it would have been somebody else, or a group of somebodies (a point that Samuelson himself made). Economists were ready for this mathematical unification, for the tools they needed to understand the world—and later change it. These same tools would transform Radford's narrative of POW camp economics into a concise set of mathematical equations.

It was an enterprise that was characterized by at least a bit of hubris: that with sufficiently well-conceived models and thoughtful application, the field could illuminate the inner workings of the economy, avoid another Great Depression, and defeat the business cycle. (Things had looked pretty promising up until around 2008.)

There's still hubris enough to go around in the economics profession today: the overstrong interpretation of mathematical models as predictive tools, in particular, is part of what's driving our grand experimentation with markets, with uncertain outcome. But if you take the models with an appropriate dosage of salt, they provide insights into the nature of our economy and a toolbox and set of intuitions for designing a better market.

Mr. Radford, Meet General Equilibrium

Samuelson's *Foundations* was really just the start. A wide-open set of problems presented itself to those inclined to work on it. And many were so inclined, leading to a generation of economists who were tackling (in many cases retackling) the field's foundational problems, now using advanced mathematical tools.

As a group, they were intellectually formidable, competitive, and, in many cases, more than a little confident of their own individual abilities. As with Samuelson, they focused on questions that were central to the development of economics as a science, but not necessarily for the reasons you might think—not just because they intended to advance the field of economics but because they were looking for challenging problems to solve, and to solve them first. It turned out that some of the fundamental building blocks of the discipline provided exactly the tough nuts they were after.

One of the foremost among this postwar group was Kenneth Arrow, a brilliant mathematical mind in search of hard economics problems to solve. And he helped solve some of the hardest, all of which related in one way or another to Radford's experiences in Stalag VII-A. But there is a difference between Radford's observation of a particular market and what Arrow and his colleagues accomplished: the mathematical modeling of the general idea of a market.

Arrow was born in New York City on August 23, 1921—another child of the Great Depression. He studied social sciences and mathematics at City College in New York and graduated in 1940. His family had lost everything during the 1930s, and his aspirations went no further than using his talents to earn a decent living. He entered Columbia University for graduate study in statistics, which started him on a path to a career as an actuary, a stable but famously dull profession. (A joke popular among accountants runs something like, "Why did the accountant become an actuary? Because he found bookkeeping too exciting.") Under the influence of the statistician-economist Harold Hoteling, he changed his focus to economics.

During World War II, Arrow served as a weather officer in the US Army Air Corps, where he focused solely on theoretical research (which led to his first published paper, "On the Optimal

Use of Winds for Flight Planning"). Arrow returned to Columbia as a graduate student in 1946, while at the same time serving as a research associate of the Cowles Commission at the University of Chicago where—before he finished his graduate work—he also became an assistant professor, a testament to the potential that senior economists saw in him.

Arrow's intellectual breadth was by no means limited to the esoteric intersections of economics and advanced math. When we opened an interview with him with a question on how he came to write his renowned 1954 paper "Existence of an Equilibrium for a Competitive Economy" (coauthored with Debreu), he immediately launched into an extended disquisition on the centuries-long intellectual history of the problem confronted by the paper, jumping from John Stuart Mill's views on economic crises in 1848 to the current state of monetary policy in America. Despite being well into his nineties at the time, he spoke one hundred words a minute in fully formed and cogent ideas, as though he'd spent the past sixty years digesting and organizing the sum total of knowledge produced by economists since 1750 (which, we suppose, he has).[18]

(One bit of unverifiable Arrow folklore dates back to the 1960s, by which time Arrow had moved to Stanford. He would often lunch with fellow faculty members, including some of the greatest thinkers of the era—physicist Marvin Chodorow, mathematician Samuel Karlin, and philosopher Patrick Suppes. They got tired of Arrow always knowing more about every subject than the rest of them put together and conspired to show him up after making an intensive study of the aboriginal peoples of Australia. They casually introduced the topic at the lunch table one day. It turned out that not only had Arrow read everything that they had spent the past weeks studying up on but had a deeper knowledge of it than the rest of them. He proceeded to hold forth, as usual.[19])

It was at Columbia that Arrow first learned of the problem whose solution would make him famous, at least among economists. The holy grail of postwar economics was proving that, in a market with "lots" of small buyers and sellers trading with one another, an equilibrium would emerge. Given the wants and desires of consumers on one side, and the resources of sellers on the other, a set of prices would arise whereby every seller could sell all he wanted and every buyer could similarly buy all she wished (given the prices that came to prevail in the market). That is, economists were aiming to demonstrate, in their newly sophisticated mathematical language, the conditions that would ensure the existence of a stable market economy.

When Arrow spoke with one of his mentors at Columbia, the great statistician Abraham Wald, about this question of proving the existence of equilibrium, he was told "it is a very difficult issue"— as in, "too difficult for the likes of you." That challenge helped spur Arrow, who went ahead and proved it anyway.

The year 1951 had seen a major technical advance that made proof of existence far easier than Wald might have realized. John Nash, the game theorist made famous by the book and movie *A Beautiful Mind*, had borrowed the fixed-point theorem of Japanese mathematician Shizuo Kakutani to prove the existence of Nash equilibrium in game theory. In Arrow's retelling, at that point it was obvious how to go about proving the existence of competitive equilibrium, and it was a race among himself, French economist Debreu, and several others to see who could do it first and do it best.

As Arrow recalls, he summarized his first attempt at proving the existence theorem in a working paper just before heading to Europe to give some lectures. Shortly after his arrival, he started getting cross-Atlantic messages via airmail from Debreu, sent from Chicago. Debreu had seen Arrow's paper. His initial note informed Arrow that he'd been doing work along the same lines, and he passed on a manuscript that contained his version of the existence proof. The next day, Debreu sent another message saying that he'd gone more carefully through Arrow's manuscript and found a mistake, and that he (Debreu) was going to try to publish his version. The *next* day, Arrow got yet another message saying that Debreu had been wrong, it *wasn't* a mistake, but that he'd found another error in Arrow's work. Arrow pointed out that Debreu had made the same mistake. Long story short, they got together, worked through their errors by making a few extra assumptions, and published the results together.

The average layreader would be unable to parse even half a sentence of Arrow and Debreu's 1954 proof. The market they describe is a highly abstract one, and truth be told, no one imagined that there had ever existed a market that looked just like the one in the "Existence of Equilibrium" paper, least of all Arrow or Debreu. This was partly because of the desire to have a clear, uncomplicated, and general theory, even if we all know it isn't exactly right (perhaps a bit of physicist envy on the part of economists).

But the focus on elegant simplicity also had a more practical purpose. To understand what's going on, you want a model that's just complicated enough (and no more complicated) to capture the essence of the problem. Architects would never build an exact skyscraper replica for stress testing. Instead, they create a computer model, and perhaps a six-foot-high mock-up to put in a wind tunnel. The models are absurd caricatures of the true skyscraper-to-be, but look enough like the real thing to help figure out whether it'll get knocked over in a hurricane.

In a sense, Arrow and Debreu's model was a stress test of the market, an attempt to understand the conditions that would guarantee that a market would arrive at that happy state where society's means and wants exactly coincide.

This may seem an esoteric point. And in a way it is. But think back to Smith's timeless description of the magic of the invisible hand: in a well-functioning market, each individual acts only in self-interest but nonetheless ends up promoting the public good. He's describing, essentially, the glories of market equilibrium: there's no way that the economy's resources could be put to use so that any one individual is better off without making someone else worse off (that is, market equilibrium is a Pareto optimum). There's no waste, no mixed-up allocations where you and I might barter my bread for your eggs to make us both happier, no company that could be more profitable by altering what it chose to produce. It wouldn't necessarily be the best of all possible worlds: there would still be rich and poor, as there was no government in the model that might right such inequities. But it would be efficient. And that was good.

With this as backdrop, the search for equilibrium takes on greater meaning. The conditions under which equilibrium exist might illuminate if and when and how the invisible hand would work its wonders. They had come a long way in loosening some of the truly outrageous assumptions of earlier existence proofs. For example, the pair had been delayed in publishing their 1954 proof because they were determined to get rid of the assumption that every consumer had at least a bit of every single commodity that was to be traded. Earlier models assumed that all our basements would be stocked at the beginning of time with little hunks of gold, copper, and steel, as well as whatever knickknacks might turn out to be valuable once trading started.

The list of conditions remained a lengthy and at times an abstruse one, however. Among other things, their proof of equilibrium involved well-calibrated, well-informed producers who converted inputs to outputs according to mathematically convenient production technologies and consumers who, in turn, converted purchases into happiness in accordance with a similarly convenient mathematical relationship. In this mathematical world, no car manufacturer ever lost a shipment of tires, and no iPhone user ever wished he could break his contract and move over to Android.

Those contributions helped Arrow and Debreu to each win a Nobel Prize, Arrow in 1972 and Debreu in 1983. As with many early Nobels in economics (the prize, which we are obliged to note is properly known as the Sveriges Riksbank Prize in Economic Sciences in Memory of Alfred Nobel, was only instituted in 1969), Arrow's 1972 award (shared with John Hicks) was very much an insider's prize. It was given for work that was fundamental to the discipline but was little recognized or even known to the general public: to quote the Nobel committee, Hicks and Arrow were honored "for their pioneering contributions to general economic equilibrium theory and welfare theory."

Was it of any practical use? Not directly, no.[20] In fact, Arrow himself turned to writing about health-care markets a few years after publishing his existence proof in part, he says, because he felt guilty about never doing anything practical.

But by laying out in precise terms what made a perfect market tick, Arrow and Debreu gave future researchers a clearer point of departure for understanding real-world markets' many imperfections—and an idea of where to start fixing them.

The Economics Counterculture of the 1960s

The mathematical revolution that reached its zenith in the 1950s set the stage for a counterrevolution just a few years later. The next generation of revolutionaries didn't abandon mathematical modeling but focused their efforts on tethering their abstractions more directly to tangible economic phenomena. In the spirit of the worldly philosophers, they brought the field of economics back in connection with the world it was meant to describe.

Many economists of this era refer to Robert Solow, another Nobel Prize–winning economist from MIT, as a source of inspiration for their own work. Solow introduced different kinds of capital—high versus low grade, for example—to models of competition, an early but critical step toward making them look more like real-life markets. Theodore Schultz, a midwestern farm boy whose father pulled him out of school after eighth grade for fear that an education would encourage him to leave the farm, further extended the Solow model after, paternal wishes notwithstanding, completing a doctorate in economics at the University of Wisconsin. The Schultz model added the notion that individual productivity could differ based on whether the individuals were, say, high school dropouts or engineering PhDs. He effectively started economics toward doing for labor what Solow had done for capital. (The fuller development of human capital theory came from another Nobel Laureate Gary Becker with his classic study of why individuals invest in education or experience and the consequences of these "human capital" investments for the economy.)

As obvious as this all seems—machines aren't interchangeable, nor are human beings—these new insights represented a real step forward for the discipline of economics. By introducing such complications, you can start to think about how the particulars of any real-world market—whether pork bellies or health insurance—would deviate from the pristine elegance of the stripped-down model of perfect competition. None of these innovations confronted some of the fundamental assumptions of market models of the '50s, particularly those around who knew what and when. As 2001 economics Nobel recipient Joseph Stiglitz put it, the glass-half-full hope of the modelers that came before him was that "economies in which information was not too imperfect would look very much like economies where information was perfect."[21]

Stiglitz and his generation were more skeptical. In their view, every market was dysfunctional in its own special way, and he and others went about showing that even a little bit of dysfunction was enough to render the deeply abstract general equilibrium models unhelpful in resolving all sorts of puzzles and paradoxes.

For instance, standard theory doesn't really allow for recessions, when, all of sudden, there's an explosion in the number of job seekers just as the fortunes of businesses collapse. Early models couldn't accommodate such ups and downs, because in a world of perfect information, there are no unexpected events that shock the economy into a downturn. As Stiglitz put it, "In the standard model . . . at the beginning of time, the full equilibrium was solved, and everything from then on was an unfolding over time of what had been planned in each of the contingencies." It was a model where on the first day, an omnipotent being created the economy, and everything that followed thereafter was preordained. Not really practical, no matter how beautiful the math might be.[22]

Confronting the uncomfortable realities of market misfires would require a different approach and a different style of economics. It was one that treated each type of market—along with its own particular defects and failures—as a largely independent exercise. You would never, for example, build a generic scale model of "City" to try to understand the urban landscapes of Cairo, Mexico City, Amsterdam, and New York. This new generation of economists wasn't going to abandon models altogether; they were necessary to understand any general issue—if you want to understand traffic patterns in Amsterdam, you would stop well short of building a full-scale model of the city.

MIT economist Evsey Domar—who rose to prominence as a mathematical economist in the 1940s and '50s—drew a comparison to the writing of a novel or play. An author doesn't observe the minutiae of everyday life when trying to tell a story: it would be pointless and hopelessly boring to sit through life's many dull moments.[23] Rather, "the construction of an economic model, or of any model or theory for that matter . . . consists of snatching from the enormous and complex mass of facts called reality, a few simple, easily-managed key points which, when put together in some cunning way, become for certain purposes a substitute for reality itself."

This new generation differed from their predecessors in believing that seeing the idiosyncrasies of individual markets necessarily involved different lists of key points to substitute usefully for reality (a theme that we'll pick up in the next chapter).

The point of all this isn't that you should know the ins and outs of general equilibrium theory but rather that economics had made an enormous transition even as the general topic area remained the same. By the late 1950s, economics was firmly mathematical, and in the years that followed, those tools proved useful not only in describing the world with greater accuracy and specificity but also in aiming to make the world a better place.

From Smith's *Wealth of Nations* in 1776 to the worldly philosophers of the nineteenth century, economists went from reasoning with words about the state of the world; to using words and math to reason about the world, sometimes reasoning clearly, sometimes obfuscating their points; to a mathematical revolution in the mid-twentieth century that transformed economics and set the stage for economics to transform our existence.[24]

3

HOW ONE BAD LEMON RUINS THE MARKET

THAT'S FOR ME TO KNOW AND FOR YOU TO FIND OUT (BUT ONLY WHEN IT'S TOO LATE)

Joel Podolny is now the dean of Apple University, heading a group within the company devoted, according to one insider, to teaching people at the company to "think like Steve Jobs." In an earlier chapter of his career, Podolny taught at the Stanford Graduate School of Business, where he shaped the thinking of other Silicon Valley entrepreneurs. Jeff Skoll, whose job as first president of eBay made him a multibillionaire, was one of them.[1]

As Podolny remembers it, the two ran into each other just before Skoll finished his MBA degree. Naturally, the question of what Skoll would be doing after graduation came up. Podolny recalls that Skoll had a number of options. He could return to the publishing company Knight-Ridder, where he'd worked as manager of internet initiatives before enrolling at Stanford. There was also management consulting, the tried-and-true path of the bright yet risk-averse MBA. Finally, Skoll described an alternative to the corporate track, which began something like, "I've got this friend who's started an online auction site . . ." and then went on to describe a rudimentary version of what would eventually become eBay.

Skoll's friend, Pierre Omidyar, was among the many entrepreneurially minded programmers hanging around Silicon Valley in 1995—still the early days of the World Wide Web—trying to figure out how to use the internet to get rich. Omidyar had founded a smallish trading site, AuctionWeb, which was outgrowing his ability to manage it as a single-person enterprise. He hoped to enlist Skoll to help him run it.

Podolny recalls telling the thirty-year-old Skoll that his Stanford degree gave him the "freedom to fail." Because middle management and consulting jobs would always be there for smart MBA grads, Skoll, Podonly said, should follow his AuctionWeb dreams. But even as he said it, Podolny remembers thinking, "What a ridiculous business model," and being near certain that in six months Jeff Skoll would be begging Knight-Ridder or McKinsey for a job.

The reasons for Podolny's skepticism lie at the very core of a new economics of markets that began to emerge in the post–Arrow and Debreu 1960s. If the math revolution that led to Arrow and Debreu's proof in the early 1950s focused on figuring out the conditions that would allow markets to work perfectly, the following generation developed models to understand what would happen when these conditions fail, focusing on what seemed like the craziest, least plausible assumptions that Arrow and Debreu needed to make their existence proof work.

This required a whole new way of constructing economic models. The development of economics leading up to Arrow and Debreu involved ever-greater generalities. But the existence proof was enormously complex already; the only way that you could introduce further complications was, paradoxically, to strip down the model to reflect a specific industry or situation—the market for health care, or bank loans, or automobiles—and explore how relaxing Arrow and Debreu's assumptions would play out in those circumstances in practice.

The 1960s approach to modeling also aided economists in further inserting themselves into public consciousness and business practice: whereas Arrow and Debreu's proof was utterly inaccessible to the general public, the models that came a generation later could more readily be translated into a few insightful bullet points. And with their focus on specific situations, economists came in ever greater contact with practitioners of commerce and public policy, with the models informing practice, which in turn fed back into the development of more reasonable and realistic models.

Many among this new generation of economists focused on the particular assumption of all-knowing buyers and sellers, which seemed not to reflect reality. What might happen, for instance, if sellers know more than buyers about what they're selling, which is true a lot of the time in the so-called real world? It turns out you end up with the economics version of the old Groucho Marx line about never wanting to join any club that would have you as a member: if someone has something she really, really wants to sell you, there's a good chance you shouldn't be buying. Economists had shown how, under these circumstances, markets come apart at the seams, which is exactly what Podolny forecast for the future of AuctionWeb.

The internet *is* rife with counterfeits and scams, which adds friction to what many hoped would be seamless exchange. In fact, the story of eBay's early days is partly about the perils of market transactions and how they undermine the fundamentalist vision of markets as *the* answer to all the world's problems. They're insights that are worth keeping in mind today, for internet commerce participants and entrepreneurs alike.

But whatever problems eBay and others encountered initially, the tinkerers and innovators of Silicon Valley did prevail. While asymmetric information—when the seller knows more than the buyer—complicates the job of turning the economy into an internet bazaar, eBay and its e-commerce brethren have found many ways to get the market to work reasonably well. And as we'll see, their successes have provided economists with yet more fodder for their model building and experiments—often from within the companies themselves.

E-Commerce Comes of Age

Skoll came to Silicon Valley just as Omidyar and others were trying to figure out how to transform the World Wide Web into something that could serve as a platform for transparent market exchange. Part of the challenge was that it was created for an entirely different purpose. The web was born as an information management system in 1989 by computer scientist Tim Berners-Lee to handle the ever-expanding and interconnected data created by nuclear researchers at the CERN laboratories where he worked as a software engineer. There was no thought of buyers, sellers, or markets.

Berners-Lee conceived of knowledge as an interconnected network, which made it possible for the web to eventually grow into communities of interlinked buyers and sellers. This might not have been possible with a different structure—if, for instance, ideas had been organized more like a library catalog, with information grouped by subject or theme. Instead, the information was organized as an organic and evolving set of hubs and connections where eventually web architects were able to swap in market participants for facts about subatomic particles.[2]

Given this origin as an information management system, it's perhaps no surprise that one early and prescient take on how the web would transform markets emphasized its role in delivering better information to consumers on product quality. This thesis of internet as market advisor was spelled out in some detail by the husband-and-wife team of political scientist James Snider and science writer Terra Ziporyn in their 1992 book *Future Shop*. They envisioned the web as essentially a vast, web-based collection of competing and personalized *Consumer Reports*–like catalogs that would make individualized recommendations for which videocassette recorder or microwave oven to buy. In a sense they predicted the advent of web-based commerce, but their vision was rather specific and limited to the market for product information: they imagined consumers would buy personalized recommendations on what to buy from companies that would spring up to provide this service. A reviewer in the *LA Times* called their arguments "well-intentioned, well-reasoned, and intentionally provocative" though involving at least "a little puffery." A more skeptical academic reviewer called their proposals "seriously flawed."[3]

Even as *Future Shop* went to press, there were already efforts to exploit the web's global network of users and pages more directly as a selling platform. In 1992, the Cleveland-based bookseller Charles Stack became the first online retailer, beating Jeff Bezos to the internet book business by at least a couple of years. The aptly named Mr. Stack and his company, Book Stacks Unlimited, offered what amounted to a mash-up of a very rudimentary online library catalog—you could only enter a single keyword, for instance, in a book title search—and mail-order business that stocked hundreds of thousands of new book titles. Why not used ones? Because in 1992, who in their right mind would dream of making an online order for a used book, sight unseen? How would you know what you were getting?

This was exactly the same concern that Podolny had about the early eBay model. As Podolny recalled, Skoll described the eBay model as "people posting things that they want to sell—I don't even remember if you could put up pictures at that time. Jeff gave the example of a baseball card, and explained that you'd put it up with an end date, wait for bidders, then whoever had the highest bid when the auction ended would get the card. I was trying to visualize this and asked him, 'So the buyer could be in, say, Kansas and the seller in San Francisco?' He said, 'Sure!' I asked him how exactly the exchange would take place. Well, either the buyer would send a check to the card owner, who would then cash the check and send the card. Or vice-versa. Either way, someone's taking a huge leap of faith by either sending off the goods or cutting a check before they know what they'll get in return. The opportunities to cheat are just so high."[4]

According to accounts of eBay's early days, Skoll himself shared this skepticism. He questioned whether AuctionWeb—or online retail more generally—would amount to much of anything (although Podolny doesn't recall Skoll expressing such doubts over small talk on the campus lawn). This might explain why Skoll initially took the job at Knight-Ridder rather than committing to Omidyar's start-up full-time. While there, his misgivings were fed by a speech he gave at a symposium on internet commerce, where he asked whether anyone in the room had ever bought anything online. Only three hands went up out of an audience of several hundred. If even those at the vanguard of tech commerce weren't shopping online, what hope was there that everyone else ever would?

Kicking the Tires

George Akerlof never set out to create the intellectual framework that helped nurture the e-commerce explosion or transform the way economists devised their theories. In the 1960s, he was just another young assistant professor trying to get his somewhat unorthodox paper on the economics of the used car market published in an academic journal.

When we spoke with him, Akerlof was a resident scholar at the International Monetary Fund in Washington, DC, where he moved with his wife, Janet Yellen, on her confirmation as chair of the Federal Reserve. When not accompanying his spouse and her Secret Service escorts to the sorts of events that the most powerful central banker in the world needs to attend, he leads a tranquil, academic existence. Unlike some other recipients of the prize, he hasn't used his Nobel to secure guru status in politics or business, nor does he chase after high-paying gigs through consulting or corporate board appointments. He seems, to the best of our observation, content pondering big questions in the relaxed and unhurried manner that's defined his career: when we e-mailed him to ask if he would talk to us about his classic paper on asymmetric information, "The Market for 'Lemons,'" he responded, "Sure, happy to talk whenever is good for you."[5]

In explaining how he came to do the work that ultimately won him a Nobel Prize, the Berkeley economist recalled his experiences as a PhD student at MIT in the 1960s (in the economics department built by Paul Samuelson). He arrived at graduate school just as economists were starting to get past the extreme abstraction that had ruled the profession in earlier decades. When initially confronted with the question of what inspired him to write about the used car market in the paper that made him famous, Akerlof didn't talk first about unemployment (a failure of standard models that has troubled Akerlof throughout four decades as an economist), or 1960s economics counterculture, or any other economic phenomenon. He mentioned a course in algebraic topology, the branch of mathematics that studies shapes and spaces and how they're transformed through stretching and bending. He took the course as a graduate student from the Harvard mathematician Raoul Bott. Why topology? "I don't know," he replied, "I just had some sense that I might get something out of the course. I wanted to be free of the current technology of the time."

As Paolo Siconolfi, a mathematical economist at Columbia University, explained to us, the value to Akerlof may not have been topology in particular but rather the way that mathematicians explore very general patterns and phenomena through example.

A topologist thinks of all two-dimensional objects as belonging to the same class of object. A square is no different from a circle: one is just a reshaped version of the other—at least topologically speaking. But a topologist (or a professor teaching the subject to those new to the field) might try to better understand the general properties of such shapes by investigating the example of a square or triangle or circle.

In writing his lemons paper, Akerlof was examining the very general market circumstance where one side of the market knows more than the other. But he did so by creating a "toy model" and then played with its implications. To stretch the topological metaphor, it was as though he wrote down a general theory of shapes, which he explored in his paper by discussing what a square looked like.

Akerlof's spare, simplifying approach captures a fundamental shift in the way economists thought about modeling, backing away from generality as an end in itself to explore concepts and ideas through models that each have their own idiosyncrasies. It was a radical transformation in economic modeling, and one that proved crucial for getting past the extreme assumptions and mathematical complexity of general equilibrium theory. Instead of altering the standard model, Akerlof introduced a new way of modeling—what's come to be called applied theory in economics—theory that actually has some ready and apparent counterpart in the real world. The shift toward more directly translating the real world into economic models also set the field up to go in the other direction: to take models and markets designed on paper and use those ideas to shape the way the world works.

(This desire to have the profession reflect more directly what we observe in reality has also contributed, no doubt, to the rise of empirical economics, which aims to use data to inform our view of the world. This empirical revolution has been powered in large part by the IT revolution and resultant computing power, which lets researchers put data to work on a scale that was unimaginable in Akerlof's time.)

Abstractions aside, what did Akerlof actually do? His classic study focused on the problems that arise in the car business as a result of a few lemons sitting on a used car lot, which he saw as an easy way into the general problem of a market with informed sellers and unwitting consumers. Akerlof's model follows exactly the logic that Podolny was relying on when he predicted, if only to himself, the failure of eBay. It also gave rise to a generation of economists and businesspeople who have traded, sometimes unwittingly, on the theory of lemons markets.

As with so many radically important ideas in economics, you don't need complicated math to understand Akerlof's argument. It's possible to grasp it with a simple example. In fact, Akerlof's analysis is only slightly more complicated than what we describe here.

Here is Akerlof's insight explained. Suppose there are two types of cars: those that work well and those that don't. There are lots of reasons some cars end up not running well; their owners grind the gears too much or don't change the oil enough or drive too fast; and some just come out of the factory assembled with less care than others. (Try googling "Friday Car" or "Friday afternoon car" or even "Friday afternoon at 4 p.m. before a three-day weekend car" if you haven't already heard the term.)

The person who has abused his vehicle or who knows from years of driving that the car doesn't run reliably knows the car is a lemon. The unsuspecting buyer doesn't. All cars, whether built on Wednesday or Friday, look basically the same. Now think of a world in which these two types of cars are owned by the same type of person: the kind that wants to sell her car. The ones that are stuck with bad cars are happy to part with their lemons for $2,000. The car owners that got decent vehicles (a cherry, as in cherry-picked) and took proper care of them will only sell for $10,000. If they can't get that much, better to just keep driving an old and reliable car than sell it and buy a new one. Buyers would be happy to pay, say, $3,000 for a fixer-upper, or $12,000 for one that turned out to be in decent shape.

In this market, there are gains from trade for both kinds of car, good and bad. A lemon owner should be able to trade his vehicle to a willing buyer for somewhere between $2,000 and $3,000, and both parties to the transaction should go home satisfied. Cherries owners should be able to get more than their walk-away price of $10,000 from buyers that are willing to pay up to $12,000 for a good car. Overall, buyers are happy, sellers are happy, and the market works its magic just as it did for the inhabitants of Radford's POW camp at Moosburg.

But, as you might already be figuring, things don't necessarily work out that way. Lemons will get traded for something in the $2,000 to $3,000 range. Not so for hopeful buyers and sellers of higher-quality cars. Think about a cherry owner. He won't part with his car for less than five figures. Suppose he puts it up for sale with a sticker price of $11,000. Now put yourself in the shoes of a potential buyer. You're happy to pay that much for a good-quality vehicle, but there's no way of telling that the car with the high sticker price isn't just a dolled-up lemon—the automotive equivalent of a pig with lipstick. A smart buyer isn't going to be willing pay more than $3,000 for *any* used automobile.

Akerlof's paper shows how this kind of reasoning can lead a market to unravel completely. Imagine, for example, there are even junkier vehicles that no one would spend more than a couple of hundred dollars on and are hard to distinguish from the $2,000 option. Then concern about quality will destroy the market even for "higher-quality" lemons.

So, in a car market where sellers don't know a cherry from a lemon, we end up in a situation where every vehicle on the lot is priced like a lemon, and "used car salesman" has come to serve as shorthand for rip-off artist. If you've ever wondered why the value of your car drops by 20 percent the moment you drive it off the lot, it's the lemons problem at work as well: what kind of seller wants to unload his purchase moments after he's paid for it? Only one who discovers that he's got a lousy car (or makes it lousy with just a few miles of driving). More importantly, because of the frictions that these gaps in information create for buyer-seller transactions, the market no longer performs its miracles of efficiency. There are people who have something to sell—a good-quality vehicle—and buyers who would happily pay the asking price, if only they could be surer of what they were buying.

But they can't, and the market collapses. This was the basis for Podony's concerns about eBay, and it doesn't just apply to used cars or e-commerce sites.

Consider, for instance, one of the dangers of rising unemployment, a topic more in line with Akerlof's larger agenda of trying to explain broad macroeconomic phenomena like recessions and unemployment that couldn't be reconciled with off-the-shelf models of competitive markets.[6]

In graduate school, Akerlof had already taken a shot at making sense of unemployment by writing down a search model where it takes some time and effort for employer and employee to find one another. He was "sort of, but not 100 percent, pleased" with this effort, which constituted his PhD thesis. Search models essentially throw some sand in the gears of the frictionless economies of Arrow and Debreu. The unemployed stay unemployed as much by choice as necessity, turning down job offers as they patiently scout out more promising opportunities: maybe something with a shorter commute, higher pay, or greater prospects for career advancement.

In Akerlof's view, this was hard to reconcile with extended stretches that many Americans spend without a job, despite a willingness to do just about anything for pay.[7] Lots of people do scan the want ads looking for something better than the burger-flipping or telemarketing opportunities that immediately present themselves. But this view of unemployment ignored many of the brutal job market realities experienced by the long-term unemployed that he felt a model should be able to explain.

That's what led him back to the market for lemons, which was a more satisfying framework for understanding why the labor market doesn't work for so many people. (It wasn't Akerlof's last word on why the labor market falls so far short of the Arrow-Debreu ideal, but it was at least a model that he found to be a lot more satisfying than anything that preceded it.).

Even if the market for unemployed workers doesn't quite collapse under the weight of "adverse selection" (the absence of higher-quality items from the market because their owners keep them), it's possible to see the connection between the markets for used cars and "used" workers: if a job applicant's previous employer didn't want to keep him on the payroll, it's worth asking why not. You can also imagine that the problem deepens the longer you've been out of work: Why on earth hasn't she found *someone* willing to give her a job, and what are other prospective employers seeing that I don't? That same logic explains why, if you're still single by the time you reach a certain age, it becomes harder and harder to convince a potential mate that there isn't something wrong with you. And so, voilà, you have markets with lots of unsold used cars and lots of unemployed people desperate for a job at any wage.

A New Economic Paradigm

"The Market for 'Lemons'" did more than just build the foundation for the field of information economics. It changed the way economists think about models. As we've seen, the lemons model doesn't talk of buyers, sellers, capital, and labor as extreme abstractions, as Akerlof's immediate predecessors had: there are cars and dealers and customers with money to spend in the used car market. It also doesn't build a model from scratch: Where did all these cars come from, and how did each dealer come to get his hands on one? Where did customers spend the rest of their time while not looking for automobiles, and why were some more interested in high-quality cars and others unbothered by a bit of engine trouble? As far as Akerlof was concerned, those weren't his problems. He wanted to understand the market for used cars (and markets for other items that had similar properties), not develop a grand unified model of the global economy.

It's hard to overstate what this shift in approach represented for the field of economics. In contrast to the steady march that had taken place toward ever-greater generalizability of models, scholars were beginning to take *specific* phenomena they wished to explore and build up models that, while still abstract, aimed to capture the essence of a real-life market.

Akerlof, with characteristic modesty, has observed that this was merely a return to the approach that iconic economists like Joseph Schumpeter and John Maynard Keynes had taken to describe the economy, where there was no pretension of modeling a complete system. Aspects of a market just drop from the sky. For instance, why do humans have the tendencies and instincts in market transactions that Keynes famously described as our "animal spirits"? Where did the entrepreneurs that wrought Schumpeter's "creative destruction" come from? In both cases, they were assumed into existence, based on shrewd observation or perhaps appeal to the work of other disciplines. (If you want to understand animal spirits or other whims of human nature, economists are probably the last people you'd want to ask.)

The journal editors and peer reviewers who read the paper only saw the square that Akerlof was describing rather than the topological insight, as it were. Akerlof's style of reality-based economic modeling was so novel that it confounded the profession's old guard. Akerlof discovered this soon after submitting his work to a leading academic journal, only to be told by the editor that they "did not publish papers on subjects of such triviality." Others thought his example was self-evident or outright wrong (as one reviewer noted, "I can see a market for used cars just outside my window"). Simple, yes, but certainly not trivial.

These reviewers and editors missed the deeper theory for which used cars were just one illustration when they should have been astonished by the profoundness of his general observations. Those observations turned into one of the most cited and important papers in the history of economics.

There are now generations of models that have built on Akerlof's basic lemons framework. But his influence runs much deeper: he essentially launched the entire field of applied theory within economics that aims to understand markets and the economy through models that are very much in the spirit of Akerlof's approach. To give just a few recent and influential examples, there are applied theory models that explain why law firms incorporate as partnerships, why individuals with preexisting medical conditions can't get insurance *at any price*, why government bureaucrats are so often unhelpful and downright intransigent. (The rest of this book comprises other canonical examples, each launching entire fields of inquiry within economics.)

Companies like eBay, Amazon, Airbnb, Facebook, and Uber employ PhD economists to more directly translate conceptual insights from Akerlof and his followers into practical guidance on how to better compete in the marketplace or, as we'll see, reimagine marketplaces altogether. (The paper's main insight is, in a sense, a warning for all businesses where information is of paramount importance: when the seller knows more about the quality of her wares than the buyer does, the market is prone to collapse.)

And all this can be traced back, in some small way, to young George Akerlof choosing to sit in on a topology class his first year at Harvard.

Adverse Selection on eBay

Despite his early doubts, Jeff Skoll did ultimately end up running eBay, which (along with other e-tailers like Amazon) has succeeded in selling on the internet only because of the enormous resources it devotes to keeping customers from getting screwed.[8] As one eBay economist put it to us, in academic parlance, "Our job is to reduce asymmetric information on eBay."

We buy much more than books (both new and used), diapers, and pet food online now. There are thriving online markets for collectibles, Chinese antiquities, and high-end automobiles. (One of the founding legends of eBay, unfortunately apocryphal, is that Omidyar created AuctionWeb to help his then girlfriend find trading partners for her Pez dispenser collection.)

At the time of writing, eBay Motors has listings for hundreds of Porsches, including several with registered bids above $100,000. Dozens of Chinese vases on eBay attracted bids in excess of $10,000 apiece. And early doubters notwithstanding, we get heaps of advice—much of it personalized—via the web on what to buy and why, if not in precisely the form that *Future Shop*'s authors anticipated.

But the story is a lot more complicated than simply a case of tech visionary Pierre Omidyar proving academic Podolny wrong in overcoming Akerlof's lemons problem. Yes, billions of transactions have occurred on eBay in the past decade. But all of the problems that Podolny foresaw have been visited upon eBay and its e-commerce competitors throughout their existence, largely because we remain a long way from the world of fully informed consumers that early web advocates anticipated.

Forget for a moment the challenges of buying and selling fine art or automobiles via the internet. Consider the seemingly straightforward online purchase of AAA batteries. You want to buy a reputable brand, so you enter "AAA Duracell batteries" in Amazon's search box. It turns out that Amazon itself doesn't stock Duracell batteries, so any search on their website yields a set of purchase options from third-party merchants that use Amazon as an online selling platform. The top listing, "The home store," gets a four-star rating overall—not bad.

But take the time to read some of the customer feedback, and your battery purchase starts to feel more like a spin of a roulette wheel. Amid the satisfied customers is a sizable minority of disgruntled ones. A user named Specklebang, for example, describes the batteries the company sent as "expired Chinese knockoffs" delivered in Ziploc baggies. Both of his complaints are echoed in the feedback of other reviewers, one of whom even claimed his batteries exploded. At this point, you might (as one of us did, having gone through this exercise himself) feel compelled to run out to the nearest brick-and-mortar establishment where you can see and feel a pack of legitimate made-in-the-USA Duracell batteries before you buy them.

It's not just batteries: in recent years, Johnson & Johnson has clashed with Amazon over its concerns that third-party sellers were selling expired Tylenol through Amazon's affiliate program, while Procter & Gamble alleged that Amazon vendors were hawking counterfeit versions of Gillette razorblades.

This sort of problem afflicts lots of categories on eBay. Most famously Tiffany, the high-end jeweler, ran their own audit of eBay listings that claimed to be Tiffany made and found that a headline-grabbing 70 percent of these were counterfeits. (Researchers at eBay question this figure and point out that the study that generated it was Tiffany sponsored.)

What's a would-be Tiffany shopper to do? Well, if you *must* buy your Tiffany tennis bracelet or key necklace online, you'd do well to check out an entry from user yvonne9903, entitled "How to Spot

Fake Tiffany Jewelry."[9] It's among the many thousands of postings from members of eBay's "Expert Community" on how not to get screwed in online commerce.

Yvonne9903's suggestions, which have been viewed hundreds of thousands of times, include some straightforward tips on avoiding some of the more obvious internet scams (all quotes are verbatim):

- ALWAYS check a sellers feedback!
- NEVER, NEVER, NEVER buy Tiffany jewlery from someone who keeps their feedback private!! That can be a HUGE red flag that they're selling fakes, or have something to hide.
- Be suspicious of any seller who states in their auction that they don't want questions about the authenticity of their item

This initial set of pointers only helps in avoiding the scams of the truly unsophisticated con artists. Yvonne9903's advice stretches to well over two thousand words and involves more time-intensive seller and listing reconnaissance like:

- Don't simply check their feedback number, but *look for past buyers who may have also bought Tiffany jewelry from them recently.* CHECK OUT PREVIOUS LISTINGS! Today I JUST found a seller who had what *looked* to be an authentic Tiffany toggle necklace & bracelet set, with a fairly decent story as to why she had these items, so I checked out past items they'd sold. GUESS WHAT? They've sold at least three identical sets in the past month!! Now what are the odds of someone having THREE sets of brand new, never worn Tiffany jewelry? Right.
- In regards to the "double heart" necklaces I've seen floating out there, be aware that the hearts should NOT BE CURVED in any way, but should be shaped JUST like the hearts on Tiffany's tag necklace and bracelet. ONLY THE LARGER, BOTTOM HEART IS ENGRAVED with Tiffany & Co. The top heart is BLANK! Also, the hearts hang at an angle from the chain, if you're looking at the necklace, the chain should go through the LEFT side of the heart. The fake one's have the chain going through the top of the hearts. Don't fall for those necklaces

that have both hearts engraved, or that have "curved" hearts, those AREN'T TIFFANY!!

To advertise her own good nature as an unpaid shopping advisor, yvonne9903 reported in 2011 that eHow.com, a how-to-do-anything site, offered to buy her advice column for a modest sum. But "after about .019 seconds of thought" yvonne9903 said no. "Why? Because I worked really hard on this guide for *you*, the ebay buyer. No way would I have taken this guide off of ebay." In an ironic final flourish, yvonne9903 also reported that plagiarized copies of her fake-spotting advice had been proliferating online and asked those responsible to *"please stop."*

The fact that such advice is even necessary is itself evidence in favor of Podolny's view that it would be hard to keep eBay sellers honest: there are lots of swindlers on the site who continue to feed off the plentiful supply of easy marks hoping for a bargain.

After the all-caps histrionics of yvonne9903's advice page, it's worth taking a step back, breathe deeply, and observe that it's not as if conniving entrepreneurs making false or misleading pitches only arrived in 1992 with the advent of the online retail. But accompanying the long and distinguished history of conmen and their gullible buyers is a parallel account of the many ways that honest dealers and shrewd consumers have tried to overcome the problems of cheap talk and false advertising (a point we return to later on). The parties that have worked to give us faith and comfort in market transactions haven't always been celebrated for their role. In many circles the term "middleman" is a dirty word for the cut of the transactions they broker (and provide assurances of quality). One promise of the web had been to cut out such intermediaries by more easily connecting buyers and sellers. Who needs an itinerant rug or jewelry merchant profiting from his position between buyer and seller without apparently making anything himself when the transacting parties could just find one another via the web?

But in many ways the internet instead brought problems of seller misrepresentation to a whole new level. It's that much easier to appear a bit too good to be true in an online ad—whether on a dating site or an eBay product listing—than in real life, especially when you extend commerce beyond individual communities to largely anonymous transactions between buyers and sellers who might (or might not . . . you never know) be in Kansas, California, or Hong Kong.[10] (Remember, as the *New Yorker* cartoon told us, "On the internet, nobody knows you're a dog.")

On Fooling All of the People All of the Time

If buyers aren't well informed, we're at least aware of our own ignorance—in part thanks to the services e-commerce sites provide (including the inimitable yvonne9903). If everyone knows that used car salesmen are peddling lemons, no one will ever get conned, right?

If only it were so.

Of course, we know *you* would never get stuck with a lemon, but consider the following study conducted by William Samuelson (son of the more famous Paul from Chapter 2) of Boston University and Max Bazerman, at the time a professor at the Sloan School of Management at MIT. The example lays bare our human inability to fully grasp the lemons problem. And even better, if you appreciate the study's lessons, you may find yourself a little less vulnerable to con artists and confidence men in the future.

In Bazerman and Samuelson's experiment, 123 Boston University MBA students were asked to consider the following situation.[11]

You're representing a major oil producer—let's call it BP—that's thinking of buying a small drilling company, Alaskoil, that's recently acquired the mineral rights to a promising property in Alaska's North Slope. The value of the acquisition depends entirely on how much oil turns out to be under the new land—something nobody currently knows. Worst case, the property is dry and it's worth nothing. Best case, it generates $100 million in profits for Alaskoil over the well's productive lifetime. There's a lot of uncertainty over whether it'll be a gusher or a dud: the well's value is just as likely to be zero, $100 million, or any number in between.

Everyone agrees that, given its superior oil extraction expertise, the value of the new well is 50 percent greater for BP than it is for Alaskoil. So while under the worst case scenario the property is worth nothing for either company, if the well turns out to have a value of $100 million for Alaskoil, it'll be worth $150 million to BP. If there's some intermediate outcome—let's say Alaskoil could make $50 million off it—it'd be worth $75 million to BP.

From all indications, Alaskoil is happy to be acquired, as long as it is at a profitable price. You need to make a take-it-or-leave-it offer *now*, before Alaskoil figures out the level of oil reserves in its North Slope property. But here's the catch: executives at Alaskoil won't respond to your bid until *after* they finish surveying the drill site, at which point they will have a precise sense of its profitability.

Thus, you as a representative of BP will not know the value of Alaskoil's property when you submit your offer, but Alaskoil execs will know its value when deciding whether or not to accept your offer. It's a classic case of the seller knowing more than the buyer at the point an offer's made.

What do you bid? To figure that out, you need to consider what you think the "expected value" of the property is—that is, what it'll be worth on average if your bid is successful. If you're like the vast majority of BU MBA students, you pick a value somewhere between $50 and $75 million—after all, Alaskoil is worth $50 million on average (recall that it's worth somewhere in the range of 0–$100 million), and if it's worth 50 percent more to BP, that means it's worth $75 million on average. So, if you bid between $50 million and $75 million, BP stands a good chance of both having its offer accepted and turning a profit, right? That seems like sound reasoning.

Not so fast. The truth is, no matter what you bid, BP can expect to lose money.

Here's the logic. Think about a bid of, say, $60 million. If, when Alaskaoil surveys its land, it finds a lot of oil (specifically, more than $60 million worth), it'll choose not to sell (in exactly the same way that better cars are kept off the used car lot). If Alaskoil takes your $60 million offer, you know that the most it could possibly be worth to the current owners is $60 million. So you have to revise your "expected value"—the amount it'll be worth on average—to $30 million. Even if it's worth 50 percent more to BP, you've still just spent $60 million on a company that's worth only $45 million.

You can pursue this logic all the way down to zero. As you lower your bid to limit the potential downside, you get stuck with an ever-worsening set of prospective purchases, should you be "lucky" enough to put in a winning bid. (Think about what would happen if you bid just a dollar: your bid only gets accepted if Alaskoil finds its wells are coming up totally dry.)

If it's hard to follow the way the market for oil companies unravels, that's exactly the point. Akerlof was right in presuming that information problems wreak havoc on markets but perhaps too optimistic in his prognosis of consumer understanding of the problem. If appreciating Akerlof's lemons model can help us make sense of how and why markets unravel, Bazerman and Samuelson's experiment highlights exactly how hard it is for your average market participant to recognize the problem.

Consumer naïveté has its upside. Today, reputation scores let a buyer on eBay distinguish, to some degree, high-quality sellers from lemons, and a seller can avoid deadbeat customers by taking payment through PayPal before mailing off the goods. As Omidyar and Skoll were getting started, though, eBay transactions involved a bigger leap of faith, and it's easy to see how adverse selection might have killed the market early on.

According to Podolny, eBay's founders took it as a testament to the fundamental goodness of human nature that eBay survived: buyers and sellers didn't cheat their customers despite the economic benefits of doing so. But consumers' failure to grasp the nuances of adverse selection may have been crucial to generating the volume of traffic required to get the site off the ground. If they'd thought hard about the lemons problem, maybe they would have found their collectibles or Tiffany earrings somewhere else. That would have prevented the site from reaching the scale it needed to survive: buyers only shopped on eBay because lots of items were posted, and sellers only posted items because lots of people bid on them, even if some ended up with lemons. In fact, the disillusioned customers who recognized they got cheated served a valuable function as well: their feedback jump-started the seller ratings that provided an early corrective to the problem of lemon vendors.

Lemons Model, Meet the Real World

Lest you think the failure to recognize lemons is restricted to low-stakes decisions like the choices of BU MBA students in lab experiments or early buyers on eBay, think again. Take the challenge of providing access to health insurance for all Americans. To ensure that insurers didn't discriminate against those in poor health, in the 1990s a number of states passed legislation requiring insurance companies to offer coverage to all applicants at prices that didn't depend on health status (although they could depend on age). So, for example, an obese and diabetic forty-five-year-old male would be offered the same menu of insurance options at the same set of prices as a healthy man of the same age. But this meant, as often as not, that health plans were overrun by obese diabetics and similar high-cost enrollees, while the fit and healthy remained uninsured at higher rates than the sick and infirm. This forced insurance companies to raise premiums to cover the costs of treatment for diabetes and so forth, thus setting off the inevitable "death spiral" of higher prices and an ever-sicker insured population.[12]

Appreciating how the lemons problem affects health markets can help explain why so many economists—regardless of political leanings—favor some version of health-care policy that *forces* every individual to sign up for insurance, albeit at the expense of taking away individual choice and autonomy, which is a much-celebrated feature of the market. By obliging the healthy to remain as buyers in the market for insurance, regulation could prevent the death spiral of ever-worsening patients and ever-higher costs from ever getting started.

It's somewhat counterintuitive, but a similar logic applies to the market for oil companies: Alaskoil executives are better off if they can convince BP that they'll decide whether to accept the acquisition offer before finding out how much oil they're sitting on. In an obvious way, Alaskoil is sacrificing an informational advantage by doing this; but the alternative is that they may get no offer at all. If they make a decision before assessing the oil content of their wells, Alaskoil's leaders may end up selling wells for less than they're worth, but just as often BP will pay tens of millions of dollars for a well that turns out to be dry. As long as buyer and seller are equally ignorant, both stick around to trade, and the market works just fine.

$$$$

The moral is that we aren't congenitally well calibrated with the right amount of skepticism in thinking about market transactions, or even in designing markets for products like health insurance that have a lemons problem. Everyone hopes for the too-good-to-be-true purchase—the undiscovered Monet at a garage sale or a discounted Tiffany necklace—and we're too willing to suspend disbelief in hopes that the unlikely will happen. But if the deal is too good to be true, you'd do well to think through why it's there in the first place.

Just to drive the point home on the perils of adverse selection, after a ninety-minute lecture on Akerlof's lemons problem one of us (Ray) used to add one final lesson: he would pull out his wallet, bulging with bills, and explain that he'd auction off all the cash in it to the highest bidder. "Who will offer $10?" Immediately half a dozen hands would go up in the air, from students at one of America's top business schools, who were eager to pay $10 for $10,000 worth of Monopoly money.

When it comes to selling lemons, you really can fool most of the people most of the time.

It's why, despite their best efforts, no amount of antifraud efforts by Amazon or eBay or anyone else will rid the world of conmen. As long as there's money to be made off easy marks, there will be operators able to separate fools from their money. And if somehow tomorrow morning we were to figure out a technology to end information asymmetry, someone else would figure out by tomorrow afternoon some way of making more of it.

4

THE POWER OF SIGNALS IN A WORLD OF CHEAP TALK

FACE TATTOOS AND OTHER SIGNS OF HIDDEN QUALITIES

When fifteen-year-old Robert Torres came home in 1977 with the letters "SF" tattooed on his left hand, his horror-struck mother, Frances Hernandez, asked him why on earth he'd gone and "marked [himself] for life." The initials served to permanently identify young Robert with the San Fers, one of the Latino gangs fighting increasingly violent turf wars in the San Fernando Valley in the late 1970s.[1]

Twenty years later, Torres was just coming off a yearlong stint in jail for violating his probation on previous drug and burglary convictions. But he had long since severed his connection to his old crew and told his mom that he was finally set on getting his life together. He didn't want to go back to jail, where he had been automatically placed in the gang unit because of the initials on his hand and had been forced to get a second tattoo reading "San Fer"—this time across the back of his neck—to prove again his loyalty to the gang. Now, on his second evening of freedom, he went in search of his ex-wife and five kids to tell them he wanted to make up for lost time.

He never made it. According to witnesses, Torres received a fatal shot to the head as he walked out of a liquor store where he'd stopped to buy some cigarettes. The killing was allegedly payback from a member of the Shakin' Cat Midgets, a gang that hadn't even existed when Torres got his original tattoo but now considered themselves rivals to the San Fers. Torres's killing was thought to be a revenge attack for a drive-by shooting that had taken place a couple of weeks earlier—when Torres was still behind bars. According to LAPD detective Bob Tauson, Torres was "just standing on the sidewalk, not bothering anybody. I guess they must have saw his tattoo."

It is easy to chalk up Torres's gang markings as a costly act of youthful indiscretion and rebellion, one with ultimately fatal consequences. As one police officer put it, "Unfortunately, this guy made a dumb decision when he was a kid." Torres had certainly paid dearly for his San Fer tats, and not only in his final efforts at cleaning up his life. In the years prior to his death, Torres had made repeated efforts at finding legitimate employment, and no doubt the SF etched prominently on his hand made him less employable.

But such a superficial evaluation does a disservice to the purposefulness and sophistication inherent in these rites of passage. Torres's tattoos had devastating consequences precisely at the point in his life when he was trying to turn things around. But some would say that is exactly what they were meant to do—pledge Torres to a gangster's life in a credible and visible way that the less committed would never choose.

If Akerlof's lemons model illuminated how information gaps can make markets disappear, the signaling model of Michael Spence—built on the foundations laid down by Akerlof—explains one way that buyers and sellers can save the market. As a result, we now better appreciate why the San Fers and other gangs insist on permanently marking new members, why Goldman Sachs and McKinsey recruit Harvard philosophy majors, and why profit-focused corporations "burn money" by giving to charity.

Cheap Talk

Compare Torres's tattoos to some other signs of commitment: the phrase "I love you" spoken above some club music at 2 a.m., or "Trust me" in an e-mail from a Nigerian "prince."

What do such assurances convey? Endearment? Faith? Honor? To an economist (and likely to you, we hope), they express nothing. They're cheap talk. Economists are hardly alone in holding this view. There's no shortage of English expressions that convey this sentiment. "Show me the money." "Actions speak louder than words." "Talk is cheap, deeds are precious." And this is just English—every language has its talk-is-cheap expression. In Spanish it's *hablar es fácil* (talk is easy); Reagan famously quoted the Russian version, *doveryai no proveryai* (trust, but verify), in describing his attitudes toward Soviet leaders during the Cold War. And as far as we know, none were coined by economists.[2]

Despite its dubious value, cheap talk is everywhere. Some might argue that most advertising is comprised exclusively of it; there's certainly no shortage in online commerce: "authentic" and "genuine" are near-ubiquitous descriptors among purveyors of Tiffany jewelry on eBay and in the descriptions of plenty of other items (baseball cards, Pez dispensers, antiquities) where one might have concerns of honest representation (calling yvonne9903!).

Why bother to make claims of honesty, love, or authenticity if they'll be heavily discounted by a skeptical counterpart in business or romance? It's because that while the upside is limited, the cost isn't just cheap, it's nil—so why not give it a try and hope there's a sucker out there who believes you. Saying such words is without cost, but if the hearer believes them, who knows, it might just pay off. It's not for us to say whether any particular eBay merchant is being truthful (but the Tiffany audit we described in the last chapter suggests many aren't); it's simply that for any given listing, rip-off artists and honest brokers face the same (negligible) cost of claiming whatever they like. The challenge facing sellers of genuine Tiffany and the buyers in search of them is to prove that they're not just full of empty words.

Around the time George Akerlof had finally gotten someone in the academic community to take "The Market for Lemons" seriously, Michael Spence was at the early stages of his PhD at Harvard's economics department. By the time he defended his thesis in 1972, he'd provided an answer to the cheap talk problem that also, perhaps inadvertently, helps to explain why Robert Torres ended up with San Fer tattooed across the back of his neck (even though we're sure Spence, a very proper and vaguely aristocratic Rhodes Scholar, never contemplated the issue of hand and neck tattoos).

Spence was interested in phenomena that appeared contrary to the predictions of standard models. Why, for instance, do prospective employees waste time at company recruiting events? It's surely not because they're learning much about McKinsey or Microsoft by doing so. And why do companies recruit out of universities that provided their students with esoteric knowledge that won't make them any more productive in the working world?

While Spence was thinking on these issues, one of his advisors dropped a copy of "The Market for 'Lemons'" on his desk, suggesting that he take a look. Spence later described the paper as "electrifying." He was impressed with Akerlof's work not because it was news to him that sometimes market participants had information that others didn't: he and his advisors had a reading group where they discussed exactly this set of issues on a weekly basis. Rather, as Spence explained in his 2001 Nobel lecture, what Akerlof had done was to go beyond the mere existence of lemons to elucidate and analyze the consequences for how markets worked and, equally importantly, how they failed.[3]

As Spence later related to us, one element missing from the lemons paper was any response by market agents—either buyers or sellers—to keep markets from collapsing. And, of course, Spence observed that in fact most markets managed somehow not to unravel in reality. (This may be in part why some academic reviewers had said the original lemons paper was trivial: they could look outside and still see a market for used cars; it hadn't unraveled in the way Akerlof's paper would suggest.) So Spence took a step back to think about what you'd actually do if you were in a market set to unravel—whether the market for used cars or employees or auto repair services—and were determined to do something to stop it.

In Spence's retelling, thinking about the problem in this way very quickly led to a resolution of market unraveling in theory, which also seemed to line up with the way markets worked in reality. In the process Spence's work helped economists make sense of a lot of the peculiar market rituals that appear in practice, particularly in labor markets, which were Spence's focus.

Spence's Nobel Prize–winning thesis focused on how good workers reveal themselves as smart or dependable, but the same lessons have been applied by economists in the decades since to understand how sellers in many markets go beyond cheap talk in proving that they're selling cherries instead of lemons.

In Spence's classic formulation, hiring a worker is essentially a spin of the roulette wheel: depending on what comes up, you might get a conscientious, productive worker or an incompetent, shirking one. (It's often hard to distinguish incompetence from deliberate obstructionism, and on some level it doesn't matter to the employer—either way not much gets done.[4])

There are plenty of steps that employers can and do take to make the hiring decision less of a gamble. They may consider, consciously or not, whether the applicant is short or tall, black or white, male or female. Based on prior experiences or stereotypes they've formed, recruiters may make a positive or negative judgment of what the applicant would probably be like once he starts showing up for work. Whether it's legal or moral (or even correct), we judge people based on all sorts of characteristics that a person is essentially born into.

Then there are the choices we make in presenting ourselves to a prospective employer: short or tall, black or white, male or female, you need to decide whether to wear a suit or jeans, or to show up clean-cut or shaggy, or, like Torres, covered in tattoos. On your résumé you can choose to offer up your undergraduate GPA, and mention that it was from an Ivy League institution, or you can avoid saying much of anything about your education at all.

You might counter that lots of these aren't exactly choices either: Harvard chooses you, not the other way around. Acing advanced calculus is similarly something that is out of reach for many, so not all of us can be a math major with a 4.0 GPA.

That's correct, sort of. But you can also think of it this way: the cost of adding a credential to your résumé or presenting yourself in a particular way at an interview is higher for some applicants than for others. In a sense, the "cost" for many of getting into Harvard and making it to graduation is infinite—it's just not within the realm of possibility. For a math whiz or a music prodigy, it may not be that difficult to get in and coast through whatever the Harvard curriculum might throw at them. A driven, conscientious, and reasonably bright young person might also put together a Harvard-worthy college application without too much trouble, relatively speaking.

In Spence's model, the same attributes that make it relatively easy to get a Harvard degree—math wizardry, drive, and diligence—are also characteristics that make for a productive employee. If that's the case, then companies will do well to hire Harvard math majors, even if no one learns anything of practical use, or even any math, at Harvard.

Why? Because a math degree from Harvard is a credible way of telling companies, "I'm smart." In contrast to just saying to a recruiter, "I'm smart," a Harvard math degree is not something that less able applicants can mimic or would even want to because the cost—in terms of work hours and psychic suffering—is too great for those lacking high-powered analytical skills.

Stripped down to its essentials, the Spence signaling model simply requires that there be a link between being productive, honest, good—anything that's a desirable, yet hidden (at least from the buyer) attribute—and the cost of doing *something*. And that something can be anything, really, as long as everyone knows it's cheap for the smart and virtuous to do it. If it were the case that the skills required to be a great computer programmer also made it easier to stand on your head, Google could base hiring decisions on whether applicants can do a headstand during an interview—only the able coders will do so. (We've heard that Stanford business school economist John Roberts used to give his students the exercise of writing down a model where only those who could stand on their heads were offered jobs.) That's why you shouldn't get a face tattoo unless you're really, really sure that gang membership is indeed for you.

So, in the market for health insurance, used cars, and any other situation where one side of the market knows something the other doesn't, the "cherries" are well-motivated to find ways of showing they're healthy, trustworthy, and otherwise better to deal with in a way that's too costly for the lemons to copy.

Signals for Everything

Economists have applied the machinery of signaling to a broad range of circumstances—some would say too broad—many of which Spence himself never envisioned. In fact, there are over ten thousand academic citations to Spence's signaling paper and only a small minority relates to labor markets.

Many applications are downright counterintuitive. It's easy to think of an Ivy League degree as a useful signal and why you'd want to get one if you could. Less so for Roberto Torres and his San Fer gang tattoo. But it's doing much the same job as the Harvard degree. What makes it hard for most of us to think of it in this way is that we're focused on the awful cost of having to go through life with dimmed employment prospects and possibly even a crosshairs on your chest.

That's exactly the point of tattoos like Torres's or those of the notorious MS-13 gang, whose members go so far as to heavily ink their faces: for most readers of this book, the cost of gang markings is much higher than it is for those committed to gang membership. At minimum, the uncommitted might consider the future cost of finding legal employment, how he'll be perceived in "polite" society, or the financial and physical pain involved in removing the words "F*** the LAPD" from across his chest. Since such tattoos make a life outside the gang world so much harder, they won't be mimicked by interlopers or, much worse, cops and informants.

(Using similar reasoning, Eli Berman, an economist at the University of California at San Diego, has argued that signaling theory is useful in explaining the terrible quality of education provided by religious schools run by ultraorthodox Jews and fundamentalist Muslims: it ensures that kids will have few options outside their communities, which also provide extensive social support for members.[5])

Lots of seemingly self-destructive behaviors can be explained this way: a new prisoner whacking his head against the wall or jabbing a knife in his own thigh may seem crazy. But he's communicating to his audience of fellow inmates that he won't mind a few cuts or bruises in a confrontation. Compared to a fresh arrival who tries to solidify his place in the prison hierarchy by "acting tough" or "talking tough," we'd suggest that, in a way, the head banger is the more rational one. At least the message he's sending is credible.

The new inmate may very well be insane, just as gang tattoos could merely be a signal of shortsightedness. You only consider the costs if you can see more than a few months into the future. Teenagers are hardly known for taking the long view, especially ones raised in drug- and gang-infested neighborhoods. Either way, though, no one messes with the crazy dude. And whether acquired through shortsightedness or more thorough deliberation, tattoos make life outside gangs so hard that it serves as an effective commitment not to defect; it's too costly to live on the outside. Robert Torres learned this the hard way.

Why do gangs in particular resort to such extreme measures? In the opening to his book, *Codes of the Underworld*, Diego Gambetta, the eminent Italian sociologist, points out the enormous informational challenges in becoming a successful criminal organization. Online shoppers have nothing on the aspiring criminal mastermind in their need for credible signals. Suppose you want to rob a bank and need someone on the inside to help you with the job. Or you want to trade a few spare bars of enriched uranium that you grabbed in the chaos of the Soviet Union's collapse for an appropriate sum of money. How do you figure out which bank teller will be a trustworthy partner and which will contact the police? Which prospective buyers are fronting for the North Koreans and which ones are fronting for Interpol? As Gambetta writes, "Given these propensities, one wonders how criminals ever manage to do anything together." Gambetta's underworld codes—the Japanese *yakuza*'s propensity, for instance, to remove a finger to broadcast the fact that you've atoned for a breach of gangster etiquette—are the subtle ways that crooks transmit their intentions credibly (very often with a subtlety that eludes outsiders) and always with a cost that makes their intentions and loyalties credible.[6]

Mixed Signals

We are steeped in market signals, online and off. The seller's challenge is making clear that a signal is credible. As buyers, we need to recognize and assess how much weight to put on them.

In Econ 101, the money-back guarantee serves as Exhibit A for conveying a quality commitment: a lemons dealer won't make such an offer since he'll have to give refunds too often. Cherry sellers can offer no-questions-asked return policies, knowing that they'll be dealing with relatively few dissatisfied customers.

Yet the merchants best known for no-risk money-back guarantees are of the late-night infomercial variety. This is where the classroom theory confronts an uncomfortable reality. The consumer advice site Adfibs.com has a page devoted to entirely to money-back scams and describes the kinds of shenanigans you might come up against in trying to get your money returned. For example, you phone customer care, where you are given a separate number for refund inquiries. This turns out to be a recording that refers you to yet another number—the original sales line where your order was first placed. A salesperson refers you on to customer care, where the loop begins anew. Or you can contact the Better Business Bureau. But for a $44.99 refund (minus, of course, a $24.99 handling fee), is it really worth the trouble?

This is all assuming that the company is still around to give you your money back by the time you realize you've been had. The kind of business for which there is truly little cost to making promises about the future is one that expects it soon won't exist.

So it seems that, on its own, your "no-risk money-back guarantee" is at best cheap talk. It may possibly even signal the opposite of what it superficially represents.

The refund pledge starts to look more meaningful when combined with some indication that the seller is in it for the long haul. A money-back promise from retailer Nordstrom has a very different resonance than for a baldness cure seen on late night TV.[7] The reputation of Nordstrom's no-questions-asked return policy has been established over decades, to the point of becoming a clichéd illustration of the lengths to which a company will go to ensure customer satisfaction. The oft-told story of a Nordie giving one of his customers a refund for tires despite the fact that the company has never sold auto products of any kind may or may not be true: in some versions the refund takes place in Fairbanks, Alaska, in others it's in Seattle; sometimes the refund is on snow tires, sometimes it isn't. But the story's tenacity (Snopes.com, a website that fact-checks urban legends, calls it "possibly the greatest consumer relations story of modern times") lends credence to Nordstrom's claims that it really means it when it promises no-hassle refunds.[8]

That's all well and good for a company that's had years to nurture customers' trust. But what about the start-up that wants prospective consumers to believe it's got a fantastic product to sell and isn't looking just to make a quick buck? One way of sending a strong signal of commitment to the long run would be to convert the company's savings into hard currency, cart it out to the street, and light a match to it. Only a company that expects to do repeat business with lots of customers is going to be willing to pay this upfront "money burning" cost.

If we don't see many companies lighting cash-fueled bonfires, economists have argued they do the equivalent—both more credibly and more publicly—through advertising. In a classic article on advertising as money burning, "Price and Advertising Signals of Product Quality," economists Paul Milgrom and John Roberts describe a 1983 ad announcing the introduction of Diet Coke: "a large concert hall full of people, a long chorus line kicking, a remarkable number of (high-priced) celebrities over whom the camera pans, and a simple announcement that Diet Coke is the reason for this assemblage."[9] They also give the example of an even more literal take on advertising as pointless destruction in a Ford Ranger ad from 1984 that "features these trucks being thrown out of airplanes (followed by a half dozen sky divers) or driven off high cliffs." In both cases, the ad is a deliberate act of pointless excess and waste—money burning.

Milgrom and Roberts, in substantiating their analysis of product launch ads as money burning, observe, "These ads carry little or no direct information other than that the product in question exists. But if that is the message being sent, these ads seem an inordinately expensive way to transmit the information. Indeed, the clearest message they carry is, 'We are spending an astronomical amount of money on this ad campaign.'" The lavish destruction of value is the only way the signal can't be copied.

Competitive signaling can lead to perverse, even destructive outcomes for the companies involved. It might help explain why, in the year 2000, nineteen internet start-ups spent millions buying advertising time during the Super Bowl. It's also telling that eight of the nineteen—including, famously, Pets.com, with its sock puppet mascot—no longer exist. Ironically, their efforts to signal they had the deep pockets and quality offerings that would allow them to be one of the survivors in the internet's winner-take-all economy may have helped to drive these big spenders into bankruptcy.[10] You might think that such a failure rate would discourage a repeat, but the trend is back: during the 2015 Super Bowl, start-ups, including Wix.com (a company that helps users build websites), and Loctite (a glue maker) spent $4.5 million for each thirty-second spot.[11]

Whether this all has the desired effect on someone in the market for a new truck or soft drink is another matter. Milgrom and Roberts provide a coherent model describing interactions among companies signaling quality to perfectly rational, albeit imperfectly informed, customers. For this to work in practice requires one further step: you need to have customers who, while encumbered with highly imperfect and often biased judgment, react in a way that's at least rational enough.

Overall, it turns out that it's a lot easier to write down a signaling model than to make one work for you in reality: a seller requires some ingenuity to find an incontrovertible commitment ("money-back guarantee, we promise" doesn't cut it), along with customers who have the sense to understand what, by driving a bunch of trucks off a cliff, Ford is trying to tell them.

Signaling Integrity

Who would you rather buy a used car from, the owner of a porn shop or a church pastor? This is *not* a trick question. The clear choice is the one who's given up worldly wealth to serve God, not the one looking to profit from what many consider an ethically dubious vocation. A God-fearing car seller won't try to profit at another's expense; the porn dealer—well, some might say that's what he already does for a living.

A lifetime's worth of devotion to prayer, poverty, and ministering to others is a credible signal of integrity, which is why, no doubt, you'd be happy to buy a used truck from Mother Teresa, were she still with us. For a deceitful salesman, the strategy of living piously is too much of a sacrifice to be worth the trouble, so it should be a signal of integrity. But this nonetheless fails the signaling test. Deep religious devotion is too costly for most honest salesmen as well. Not only that, in most cases, it's also too hard for customers to see. How can you show such faith in a way that can't be insincerely copied? A religious necklace or a Bible on your desk won't do. If the signal is just a *claim* of religiosity, we're back to cheap talk, same as if a used car salesman assures you that the car you're looking at was driven by an elderly woman only to church on alternating Sundays.

What's needed is to scale back the strength of the signal and convert it into a form that is less prone to misrepresentation. Instead of "burning time" at church, why not "burn money" by giving generously to religious or other social causes? Even better, why leave any ambiguity about the link between your displays of charity and your commercial interests when you can donate a portion of company profits to the church or some other charity?

Lots of businesses publicly trumpet their philanthropic commitments, generally in areas that have nothing to do with the products they sell: Goldman "Vampire Squid" Sachs—blamed by many for helping to fleece investors during the financial crisis—funds an initiative to help poor African women become entrepreneurs. Target builds school libraries. GE funds community health centers. And we're not talking chump change, either: companies are spending hundreds of millions of dollars apiece to make the world a better place, and then even more to tell us about it.[12]

There are surely many reasons why companies act like do-gooders (and want everyone to know it): Milton Friedman, a champion of free-market economics if there ever was one, argued that it's primarily the result of corporate executives frittering away shareholder dollars on their own pet charities. In this view, corporate charity is a sign of a poorly governed organization. Friedman also acknowledged that customers may also get some extra satisfaction (and hence pay more) when they buy from a company that shares their concerns for bettering the environment or fighting poverty. This "warm glow" view would suggest that a company would want to show it cares if its customers (or employees) themselves do.

As we've already observed, it's always *possible* to write down a signaling model for everything, from standing on your head in a Google interview to this latest example of corporations writing checks to the Red Cross and other charities. How can we tell if what's possible is in fact what's going on in reality? Are companies using charity to signal that they're not the type to screw their customers? And if so, do their customers actually understand what companies are trying to reveal through their philanthropy?

One of us (Ray), together with colleagues Daniel Elfenbein and Brian McManus, has collaborated with eBay on a study aiming to understand what motivates sellers to give a fraction of their sales proceeds to charity. The findings come down squarely in favor of the signaling model of corporate giving.

Through its Giving Works program (now called eBay for Charity), eBay sellers can give a fraction of an auction's proceeds directly to charity. The seller gets to choose the organization that receives the donation and the percentage that they get—anything between 10 and 100 percent, in 10 percent increments. eBay takes care of actually making the donation, so a buyer can be sure that the promise is legit—there's no issue of cheap talk here.

What's nice about eBay as a research platform is that its sellers are constantly experimenting with new business opportunities to test out what works and what doesn't. And so it went with Giving Works. The program began in 2003, and in the years that followed sellers ran millions of miniexperiments to see how bidders would respond to charity tie-ins. In particular, they put up nearly identical listings, same title, same listing price, and so forth, distinguished only by their Giving Works status. So, by comparing the results of charity versus noncharity listings in groups of otherwise identical auctions, we can get a sense of whether there's a premium to charitable giving and whether it really serves as a signal in Spence's sense.

There is at least some benefit to doing good. A Giving Works item advertising that 10 percent of proceeds will be given to charity is nearly 20 percent more likely to sell than its noncharity twin, and if it sells, you can expect it to go for a price that's about 2 percent higher. (Items where 100 percent is donated to charity—hardly a sustainable business strategy—are nearly 50 percent more likely to sell and get bids that are 6 percent higher.)

But not all sellers benefit equally. Inexperienced sellers, with little feedback or track record as reliable vendors, profit much more from their charity tie-ins—a boost in sales probability of more than a third and final bids that are 4 percent higher. Those with long and unblemished sales histories don't benefit from charity tie-ins at all.

How does this fit with the various theories of corporate philanthropy? Friedman's money-wasting view of charitable giving would predict that charity wouldn't generate benefits for any sellers. It might make the seller happy, but why should his customers care? Under the "warm glow" hypothesis, all sellers should see some return on their charitable donations, yet the large, well-established sellers don't see any. So neither of these theories is consistent with what we observe in eBay auctions. The data best fit with the charity-as-signal view of philanthropy: if the type of seller that "wastes" money by giving to charity is also the type that won't cheat his customers, this signal is much more useful for new sellers than for experienced ones, whose history of positive feedback already serves as a credible sign of dependability.

If young sellers generate more sales at higher prices by tacking on charitable contributions to their listings, why wouldn't all of them, honest and devious alike, do it? That goes back to the very basic signaling principle that the "bad type" of seller won't *want* to copy the signal because it's too costly. This too fits with the numbers: it turns out that the benefits—in terms of moving inventory and generating higher prices—aren't enough to cover the 10 percent contribution (or any other contribution level). An entirely venal merchant would be better off just taking a lower selling price but keeping it all for himself, while the seller who cares about others doesn't mind lowering his revenue a bit to make the world a better place.[13]

It also turns out that buyers are entirely rational in interpreting philanthropy as a signal of trustworthiness, even if they don't consciously think about it that way. While eBay participants observe each other's public feedback ratings, these are often quite noisy. (You can see this at other online platforms like Amazon, where some one-star reviews of books focus on problems like shipping rather than the quality of the book. On eBay, unsatisfied customers often leave no feedback at all.) An additional measure of a seller's reliability is the number of times that buyers have lodged private complaints with eBay, owing to issues like delayed deliveries, poor packaging, and the receipt of items that differ from the ones that were advertised. If the two parties are unsuccessful in resolving their differences, eBay registers an unresolved dispute on the transaction. About 1 percent of eBay sales ultimately end this way. But it happens a lot less—about half as often—for sellers that frequently advertise charity tie-ins with their listings.[14]

Every Market Is Dysfunctional in Its Own Way (though some more than others)

What do we take away from the eBay experiment? There's the narrow message for the value, however limited, of corporations' philanthropic efforts. But there's also a broader lesson about the value that the models of Akerlof and Spence have brought to our understanding of markets. The signaling game involving eBay sellers and buyers is a complicated and subtle one. Yet it plays out with remarkable adherence to the script laid out by Spence in his landmark paper nearly half a century ago. Thanks to his work, we now understand the nature of market imperfections and appreciate the creative solutions that have developed in response a great deal better. Face tattoos and deliberately wasteful Super Bowl ads make a little more sense.

There's a yet broader lesson too: markets fail, as do models of markets. Akerlof and Spence could explain many aspects of the world that eluded the more abstract modelers who preceded them, but economists are still confronted by a multitude of remaining puzzles about markets and the economy that aren't resolved by implicating lemons or signals. These include the enduring and very basic question of why there are recessions. We may understand this puzzle, which has motivated Akerlof in his research to this very day, somewhat better than we did in 1960. Yet Akerlof would be the first to agree that we've got a long way to go—none of the "toy models" that applied theory has offered up come close to cleanly resolving this gap in economic understanding. At the same time, such failures shouldn't overshadow the considerable successes of these pioneering models and the field of applied theory that they spawned.

In a similar vein, neither Akerlof nor Spence would want to throw the perfect markets models of Samuelson, Arrow, & Co. on the scrap heap of failed intellectual endeavors. It is with good reason that, to this day, every PhD student in economics begins his or her training with an intensive study of Arrow and Debreu's general equilibrium model. It helps you to develop a better intuition for the intricate links and interactions among the various markets that comprise their abstract yet complete economy. And you appreciate better when straightforward markets and their representation in Arrow's or Samuelson's theories are "good enough" despite the gaps between the math and reality.

Even Joseph Stiglitz, among the sharpest critics of neoclassical economic models (and also their fundamentalist proponents), acknowledged the Pandora's box that's opened when you depart from the standard model's assumptions about perfect information and rational behavior. As Stiglitz, who shared the 2001 Nobel with Spence and Akerlof, observed in his Nobel address, although there is only a single way that information can be perfect, there are an infinite number of ways it can be imperfect.

To put it another way, it's easy to conceptualize markets where we all have complete knowledge of prices, quality, and everything else. But once we recognize the existence of imperfect information or misunderstandings, we have to specify, even at a first pass, who knows what and when. But it doesn't end there. Consider the lemons problem. Akerlof's model is premised on the notion that sellers have information that buyers don't, and further *that buyers actually know what they don't know*. We already saw that that doesn't appear to be the case: lemon vendors dupe buyers all the time. If they didn't, no one would need yvonne9903's guide to buying real Tiffany jewelry. And if buyers don't realize what they don't know, you need to ask what sellers believe about buyers: How naïve do they think their customers are? And do they price accordingly? The "he thinks she thinks he thinks she thinks" goes on forever.[15]

As you move from market to market, the answers to such questions are likely to change: the market dysfunctions faced by Bank of

America in structuring loan contracts are distinct from those faced by Aetna in designing health insurance offerings. If you're going to understand the market for banking or insurance, you'd better model them differently.

One of the key tenets of economic doctrine is that there is no free lunch. That is certainly the case for the modeling shift driven by Akerlof, Spence, Stiglitz, and others. No doubt something's been lost as economics engages more with the complicated realities of markets: it's become a discipline devoted less to elegant theorizing and more to guesswork and tinkering, guided (sometimes loosely) by a set of economic ideas.

In the good old days when economics was still a pristinely mathematical discipline practiced exclusively in the safe confines of academia, there was little risk that economists would make much trouble. Nor was there much chance for them to do any good. The pioneers of information economics set the profession on a path to better describing the nature of markets, which has in turn led the current generation to turn its attention outward to dabble in the design of markets and policy.

A great many applied theorists and empirical economists are, together, able to match theories up to data they can use to evaluate how they perform in practice. We hope that the iterative process of theorizing and testing of theories in the field and the reformulating of theories (a process of experimentation that we're in the midst of) will make it more likely that economics' increased influence on the world is ultimately for the better.

5

BUILDING AN AUCTION FOR EVERYTHING

THE TALE OF THE ROLLER-SKATING ECONOMIST

In the fall of 2006, the Japanese baseball phenom Daisuke Matsuzaka announced his interest in moving to the American big leagues. Lots of teams were keen to add Matsuzaka, a seven-time Gold Glove winner for best pitcher in Japan's Nippon League, to their rosters. The Yankees—the richest team in Major League Baseball (MLB)—were sure to go after him. Another deep-pocketed team, the Boston Red Sox, had a hole in its pitching rotation and was widely assumed to be desperate to sign the right-hander. There were likely half a dozen other teams that had some cash on hand and were also short enough on pitchers to be interested.

But there was a catch. Matsuzaka still had two years left on his contract with the Seibu Lions. Before any team could even start negotiating with Matsuzaka's agent, the Red Sox would need to pay the Lions to release him from his contract.

This was a result of the "posting system" created in the late 1990s, under which a Japanese player hoping to move to the United States would notify his team of his intentions.[1] Each interested MLB team had one chance to put in its best offer—a so-called sealed-bid auction. The highest bidder would win the right to negotiate a contract with the player. If the negotiations didn't lead to an agreement within thirty days, the player would return to his team in Japan, and no money would change hands. If the deal got done, the winning bidder would be on the hook for the posting fee to the Japanese team, in addition to whatever salary the team had agreed to pay the player.

At the time, word in the box seats was that the Red Sox were determined to beat the Yankees along with the other six teams that ended up submitting offers. But even if you really want to win, you still don't want to write a check any larger than you have to. As an MLB insider told us, "Overpaying for a player is a fireable offense." And therein lies the tension in an auction that's set up like the posting system: the risk of losing versus the risk of paying too much.

Red Sox owner John Henry might have been guided by looking at what Japanese players had gone for in the past. Except there was already a consensus that Matsuzaka's contract would take posting fees to a level they'd never seen before. The Seattle Mariners' $13 million bid for Ichiro Suzuki's contract was the highest posting fee ever paid, while, in Henry's words, "We assumed a few teams would try to blow all the other teams out of the water. We didn't know if that would represent 30, 40 or 50 million."[2]

As Henry's observation also makes clear, it wasn't enough for the Sox to think about their own need for a great pitcher. They also had to know how desperate *other* teams were for a pitcher. Beyond that, they needed to consider how much cash the teams with holes in their rotations had to burn on a new contract. It had very different consequences for the Red Sox if those with gargantuan budgets like the Dodgers or especially the Yankees (whose payroll reliably tops $200 million each year) were all in, or just baseball paupers like the Tampa Bay Devil Rays (2006 payroll: $35.4 million) and Miami Marlins (a paltry $15 million). A bidder even had to think through how desperate another team might be to ensure that Matsuzaka never left Japan. Rumors circulated at the time that a team might put in a shill bid without any intention of signing a contract, just to ensure that the ace went back to the Lions.

In the end, Henry felt the risk of losing Matsuzaka outweighed the risk of overpaying, so the Sox went high, offering $51,111,111.11 to the Lions for the right to make an offer to Matsuzaka. (Henry said his lucky number was 11.) They won and signed the pitcher to a six-year, $52-million contract and forked over the $51,111,111.11 posting price to the Lions. Matsuzaka went on to have two strong seasons with the Red Sox before getting injured and, ultimately, demoted to the minors, then traded to the struggling New York Mets.

But well before Matsuzaka's ignominious fall, the Boston papers were full of the Red Sox's buyer's remorse as the team impatiently counted the days to Matsuzaka's contract expiration. That the Sox had paid $20 million more than they'd had to get to him made it all the more bitter: Henry was right that other teams would make aggressive offers, but none was anywhere near as aggressive as the Red Sox. The next highest bid turned out to be $30 million, not $50 million.

This was neither the first nor the last time that the "lucky" winner of a contract with a Nippon League player would be filled with regret. With all but the most deep-pocketed of teams leery of overpaying for Japanese contracts, by the time Matsuzaka's Red Sox contract was set to expire in 2012, the entire posting system was on the verge of unraveling.

All this naturally got MLB management thinking about how the system could be tinkered with. Given the brilliant minds that have applied themselves to matters of economics and commerce, shouldn't there be a better way?

It turned out there was, in the form of a mechanism that had been designed over a hundred years ago by stamp dealers to sell collections via mail-in auctions and that had been independently discovered and analyzed by a brilliant Columbia University economist nearly half a century before Matsuzaka's ill-fated sale to the Red Sox.

Curiously, this different approach to auctions was almost *exactly* the same as the standard sealed-bid auction, with one small twist. Instead of paying the winning bid, the auction winner pays the price offered by the runner-up. But that one small tweak to the auction rules turns out to make a bidder's job a lot simpler, so much so that just a dozen or so years ago—as the internet revolution was gathering momentum—some thought that it would revolutionize the very nature of commerce.

Auctions markets were hardly new—to say the least. They existed back in the fifth century BC, when Roman historian Herodotus describes descending price auctions (where the price starts high and is gradually lowered until a bidder jumps in to purchase the item) as the mechanism of choice for marrying off young well-to-do Babylonian women. (Descending price auctions are still in use today to sell flowers in Holland; as a result, they're called Dutch auctions.) Auctioneers have experimented with all sorts of different rules and protocols over the centuries. There are Japanese auctions, reverse auctions, double auctions, continuous double auctions, Yankee auctions. In a Scottish (or time-interval) auction, all bidding must close within a prespecified time period. In seventeenth-century England, a variant on the Scottish auction was used where the time of the auction's close was uncertain, dictated by the exact moment when a candle of, say, an inch in length burned out ("candle" auctions are still used to sell wine in France and for government procurement contracts in Brazil).

Auction fads waxed and waned, and no wonder—there was no way of really assessing whether one method was better than another, beyond the proceeds of last night's or last year's sales. What auctioneers needed was a model that could rate (subject, naturally, to a list of assumptions about sellers and bidders) one sale method against another based on the odds it would generate a sale, the price it would likely fetch, and the likelihood that the item up for bid would make it into the hands of the bidder who valued it most.

There is now an entire discipline within economics, called auction theory, that provides frameworks and guidance to auctioneers and bidders alike, who previously had to rely on gut instinct. The field was launched by a paper that set out to explain why a second-bid auction was the best way to sell Matsuzaka's contract and many other things as well.

The Penny Black

Before we turn to the theorist who revolutionized auction theory, a little history is in order. The possible solution to MLB's auction problem began in 1840 when Great Britain issued the world's first postage stamp, the Penny Black.[3] Collecting stamps quickly became a popular pastime, and various businesses sprang up to serve hobbyists. Stamp catalogs, at first listing only a particular dealer's inventories, arrived in the early 1860s and soon evolved into comprehensive compendiums of all existing stamps along with some idea of what their prices should be. Especially in these early days, but still true today, the value of a stamp is subject to lots of uncertainty. There are infinite permutations of quality. Is a particular stamp, in philatelic parlance, fine, very fine, or superb? And if short of superb, what is the nature of the defects? A thinness in the paper? A blemish from poor handling?

Given uncertainty over what a "very fine" Penny Black was worth (not to mention uncertainty over what a listing of very fine might mean), sellers used something called an ascending price English auction, to aid in what economists call price discovery. This is the scene that most of us have in mind when we picture an auction: the gavel-wielding auctioneer at Sotheby's or an estate sale and paddle-waving buyers who signal their willingness to pay the ever-escalating prices called out by the auctioneer, until the familiar "going once, going twice" and the slam of the gavel indicate a sale to the highest bidder.

If a seller doesn't know what a stamp's worth, an English auction is a wonderful mechanism for finding out. You don't set the price too low and hand a bargain to the first customer through the door, and you don't get left with inventory because prices were set too high. By definition the sale price is what the market will bear. (The seller can add a reserve price to ensure that the seller doesn't part with his stamp for less than it's worth to him, if that's all that buyers are willing to pay.)

From the perspective of early stamp auctioneers, one major downside of English auctions was the way it limited potential buyers to those who could make it in person. Today, you can easily log into the Sotheby's website to follow along and bid at home. But at the time of these early stamp auctions, the telegraph had only just been invented. Out-of-town collectors had to mail in their bids, and auction houses needed to come up with a way of allowing mail-in bids to compete alongside live participants.

One stamp dealer, William P. Brown of New York City, described the process they devised:

> That out-of-town collectors may have equal facilities for purchasing with city collectors, bids may be sent to the auctioneers, Messrs. Bangs & Co., or to William Erving, P.O. Box 3222, N.Y. City, who will either of them represent their bids the same as

though they were personally present, and without charge. Thus, supposing either of these parties receives two bids on one lot of 20 and 25 cents apiece, they would start the lot at 21 cents, at which price it would be given to the person sending the 25 cent order, unless some one present advanced, when they would continue to bid, stopping at the limit of 25 cents . . . Persons sending bids should give the number of the lots and the highest price they are willing to give, when the lot will be bought for them as low as possible consistent with the representation of other bids.

In a live (first-price) auction, a bidder keeps raising his paddle until the price goes above what he's willing to pay for the lot that's up for bid. And what price do we expect the winner to ultimately pay? If there are just two bidders who value the lot at 20 and 25 cents, respectively, the first will stay in the running until the price hits 21 cents, at which point the gavel will fall. The lot goes to the buyer who values it for more, who gets the lot for "close" to the runner-up's walk-away price. The same is true for any number of bidders—the raises continue until the price is just above the runner-up's price, which is when the bidding (and the auction) will come to an end.

In the case of just two bidders, this is essentially no different from the outcome that Brown describes for write-in bids. The high bidder gets the lot for slightly more than the runner-up's price. While Brown goes on to explain how write-in buyers compete with live ones, you could imagine just lining up a set of write-in bids from lowest to highest and awarding the lot to the highest bidder, at a price that is just above the runner-up's bid. You'd get rid of the hassle and expense of running a live auction, taking sealed bids from locals and out-of-towners alike, and could expect the result to be exactly the same. (Well, almost—we'll come back to some of the differences later.)

And thus the mechanism that we now know as Vickrey auction was born.

The Roller-Skating Father of Auction Theory

William Vickrey, like other market revolutionaries we've described thus far, won a Nobel Prize for his efforts.

He also has the near-unique distinction of dying well before receiving his prize. Just days after the award announcement, in 1996, Vickrey drove his car off the road near his home in Harrison, New York. Emergency responders arriving on the scene found his already lifeless body slumped over the steering wheel. Researchers tend to reminisce, pen memoirs, and trace their intellectual development only *after* becoming Nobel laureates, often in preparing their autobiography for the Nobel committee. Vickrey never had that chance, so in his case, we know relatively little of his upbringing, or his own sense of the development of his various path-breaking ideas.

According to longtime friend Ronald Findlay—who taught at Columbia with Vickrey throughout his career—Vickrey didn't leave behind any clues among his colleagues. "Who knows what his thought process was?" says Findlay. He was a man of relatively few words in both his writing and presentations: his theories were rarely accompanied by recollections of whatever observation first prompted it.[4]

But it was clear from his choice of problems that—as with other leading figures in the new economics of markets—he was very focused on solving practical questions. At the invitation of General Douglas MacArthur, he accompanied his mentor Carl Shoup to postwar Japan to redesign the country's tax code, devising a system that remains in place today. He had a strength of conviction in his theories and lobbied for them tirelessly. (One of his passions was a plan to allow for the "cumulative averaging" of payments to the IRS that, he claimed, could revolutionize taxation. As far as we know, it has yet to be adopted outside Vickrey's home country of Canada, and even there it's used only for fisheries and farming.) According to Findlay, the Nobel was meaningful to Vickrey *only* because it would give him a prominent platform to promote his efficiency-enhancing policy innovations.

Vickrey was no less focused on efficiency when it came to his own life. Everyday decisions presented a series of optimization problems to be solved. Findlay, like others at Columbia at the time, recalls seeing Vickrey streak by on roller skates on his way up Claremont Avenue. Jacques Drèze, one of his graduate students, reminisced some years later about his first encounter with Vickrey when, on his way to class one September, he was "overtaken by a tall gray-haired man rollerskating at good speed with a bulging briefcase under one arm and under the other a three-sided cardboard box spun with colored threads" (the latter a homemade teaching prop used to illustrate the economic concept called "indifference surfaces").

A few weeks later, Drèze worked up the courage to ask Vickrey why he got to work in this unconventional manner. Vickrey explained that he had solved the dynamic programming problem to optimize the "joint choice of residence and means of commuting." The solution involved living in the bedroom community of Harrison and traveling to Columbia's Manhattan campus via commuter train to the Harlem station, then roller-skating up Claremont Avenue to his economics department office. He wondered why his colleagues hadn't reached similar conclusions.[5]

Economists often model the world as a fully optimized place, and Vickrey was perhaps irked that his fellow economists weren't practicing in their private lives what they preached as a profession. Much of his work involved observing apparent deviations from optimized efficiency and then offering solutions. Legend has it that he came up with his model of congestion pricing—which allows prices to fluctuate in real time as a function of whether extra customers are overloading capacity—while sitting on a near-empty late-night commuter train to Harrison. He rightly pointed out that he would have made life less pleasant for others if he'd gone home at five, when he might've taken another passenger's seat, or been forced to sit on another customer's lap. So why was he paying the same price for his 10 p.m. train as the travelers crammed into one at rush hour? By his reasoning, the late-night fare should be far less, perhaps encouraging more commuters to follow his lead in waiting a few hours before riding home.[6]

(That penchant for optimization might have contributed to his death as well. Following the same logic as his commute to Harrison on the train, he only drove on the interstate at night, when it was relatively empty. Had he been driving during the day, in traffic, it's conceivable that someone might have been able to help him.)

Vickrey's classic auction study similarly began with a precise explanation of what was wrong with the standard first-price sealed-bid auction that was standard practice in procurement auctions for everything from highways to school supplies, the same mechanism that was used to sell Matsuzaka's contract. By the time he was done, he'd unwittingly reinvented the stamp collectors' auction of choice and laid the foundations for the field of auction design in the process.

Vickrey described what he thought was a better way: the *second*-price sealed-bid auction, which is now known simply as a Vickrey auction. Then he proved mathematically that it just might be the best of all possible auctions that one could devise. He changed the auction industry from one that relied on an ad hoc choice of format to one built on design and optimization—a microcosm of economists' larger role in society.

Bidding What You're Willing to Pay

It seems such a small tweak to the way a sealed-bid auction is run: the high bidder pays the runner-up price rather than his own. Once the bids are in, it may or may not have a major impact on how much the seller gets: it depends on the gap between the top two bids. To appreciate the difference—and why, in a sense, Vickrey's paper launched the field of auction theory—you have to put yourself in the shoes of a buyer before she's submitted her bid, knowing that if she wins, she'll pay the second highest bid rather than her own.

Consider how it would have simplified John Henry's job in making an offer on Matsuzaka. Suppose, for the sake of argument, that Henry set the value of the right to negotiate with Matsuzaka at $60 million. That is, for a price of $60 million, he'd take it. If it were a dollar more, he'd walk away. (Of course, we'll never know what his walk-away price was, beyond the fact that it was above $51,111,111.11.) In a first-price auction, we've already seen that it's not clear where Henry should set his bid—sure, it should be less than $60 million, but how much less? For each dollar you drop your bid, you're less and less likely to come out on top. But then again, you're a dollar richer if you do.

In a second-bid auction, there would've been no such uncertainty as to what Henry should've bid.

Start by asking whether it could've made sense for Henry to bid *more* than $60 million, just to make sure he won (and knowing he wouldn't have had to pay the full amount anyway). The answer is no, never. To see this, think of any bid above $60 million—say $65 million. There are a couple of scenarios that could arise, depending on what other bidders do. Either the runner-up's offer is less than $60 million, in which case there's no difference between bidding $60 versus $65 million—either way you pay less than $60 million (the runner-up's bid). Or the runner-up bids more than $60 million—let's say $62 million. Then your $65-million bid puts you on the hook for $62 million for something that you'd decided wasn't worth any more than $60 million to you in the first place. Not worth it.

What about bidding less than $60 million, in the hopes of getting a bargain? In the actual posting auction for Matsuzaka, the second bid turned out to be $30 million, so you're no better (or worse) off bidding $50 million or $40 million or even $30,111,111.11—as long as you've put in a bid above the runner-up's, you're the winner at a price of $30 million. This outcome only flips when you put in an offer so low that it drops below the runner-up's, in which case you miss out on a contract negotiation that you thought was worth $60 million that you could've gotten for a mere $30 million.

Exactly the same logic applies for any runner-up bid that's under $60 million. If it had turned out that the Yankees had bid $20 million instead of $30 million, you're still no better off lowering your bid from the full $60 million the contract was worth to you. The amount you ultimately have to pay drops along with your competitor's bid, not your own.

This is what makes a second-price sealed-bid auction so special: it has the amazing property that, under a wide range of circumstances, the only task confronting a prospective bidder is figuring out how much she'd be willing to pay for whatever is on offer, writing that number on a piece of paper, and sending it in. John Henry doesn't have to think about what Matsuzaka is worth to any team other than his own (or think about what they think he's thinking); he just bids whatever he decides the player's value is to the Red Sox. And he never would've gotten that sinking feeling of having overpaid: as the bids were unsealed, he could've follow along at ease with the knowledge that he wouldn't have to pay more than what was required to win.

Finally, a Vickrey auction is also "socially efficient" in the sense that, if all participants bid their own valuations, by definition the high bidder is the one who values it the most. By contrast, the social efficiency of a first-bid auction can be undone by a timid offer from a high-value bidder or a particularly aggressive bid from a lower-value one.

Thus, a Vickrey auction achieves the holy grail of efficiency, and does it through a mechanism that's transparent and straight-forward. If MLB management knew about William Vickrey, per-haps the Japanese posting system wouldn't have been in crisis.

You might have the impression that the seller makes out badly in a second-price auction. After all, in using a first-price rather than second-price auction for the sale of Dice-K's contract, it looks like Boston's loss is the Seibu Lion's gain: an extra $20,111,111.11 to be exact. But this fails to account for the fact that all teams might have bid more aggressively if they'd known that they would be pay-ing the second highest bid if they won, rather than their own. That is, the auction rules change the bids that come in, and one of the points of a second-price auction is that it makes for higher bidding. Besides, it was concerns about overpayment that led to the crisis in the posting system in the first place: if the auction system breaks down completely, it isn't good for anyone.[7]

Johann Wolfgang von Goethe, Amateur Auction Theorist

It turned out that stamp collectors weren't even the first to beat economists to the Vickrey auction. They were already anticipated, at least in spirit, by the German writer Johann Wolfgang von Goethe forty years before the Penny Black appeared.

Like many a temperamental and idealistic artist, Goethe had an uneasy relationship with money. He was on the one hand dis-dainful of the profit motive (he once wrote to a publisher, "I look odd to myself when I pronounce the word Profit"), while at the same time anxious that his worth be recognized. And no one likes to be taken advantage of; he wanted to ensure that he got his fair share from the fruits of his labors.

Goethe employed various ruses and strategies to ensure that his more materialistically minded publishers didn't exploit him. Among them was what is believed to be the very first Vickrey-style auction.

Goethe wasn't planning on awarding the manuscript for his epic poem, *Hermann and Dorothea*, to the highest bidder. He wasn't even all that interested in how much he got paid for it; if he had been, he would surely have chosen some other negotiating tactic.

As Goethe described to Mr. Vieweg, his publisher, in a letter dated January 16, 1797, "I am inclined to offer Mr. Vieweg from Berlin an epic poem, Hermann and Dorothea, which will have approximately 2000 hexameters. . . . Concerning the royalty we will proceed as follows: I will hand over to Mr. Counsel Böttiger [Goethe's lawyer] a sealed note which contains my demand, and I wait for what Mr. Vieweg will suggest to offer for my work. If his offer is lower than my demand, then I take my note back, unopened, and the negotiation is broken. If, however, his offer is higher, then I will not ask for more than what is written in the note to be opened by Mr. Böttiger."

German economists Benny Moldovanu and Manfred Tietzel stumbled upon Goethe's negotiation with Vieweg and documented it in the *Journal of Political Economy* in 1998. According to Moldovanu and Tietzel, scholars had treated Goethe's proposition as among the enigmas left behind by one of history's greatest literary figures, whose every word and action have been scrutinized and dissected in the nearly two hundred years since his death.

But the economists argue that there's no mystery to Goethe's choice of mechanism. The author wanted to know how much he was worth to Vieweg (perhaps with an eye to extracting higher royalties from his publishers over the longer run), and he devised a Vickrey-style "auction" to get Vieweg to tell him.

To understand why this was so, it's useful to have a bit of background on the eighteenth-century book market. Today, writers are almost always paid royalties based on the number of books sold. If some book sells a hundred thousand copies, the author's take will be, to a first approximation, a tenth of what it would be if it sold a million. Authors trust publishers to report these figures honestly and put their faith in the US legal system to mete out punishment via class-action lawsuits if they don't. There are myriad ways of checking up on sales: publishers' numbers are checked by an independent auditor, and authors can look for discrepancies via Amazon rankings or by using independent sales data.

None of this was available to Goethe in 1797, leading him to muse some years later that "the publisher always knows the profit to himself and his family, whereas the author is totally in the dark." (Goethe referred to this asymmetry as "the main evil" of publishing.)

These problems were aggravated by the near-absence of copyright protection at the time. A best seller could be expected to spawn an abundance of pirated versions, so publishers did their best to keep their successes to themselves. This lack of intellectual property protection led to further conflicts of interest and opinion between authors and publishers: writers sometimes tried to sell near-identical editions of the same title to multiple publishers, and it was standard practice among publishers—even respectable ones—to have multiple print runs without an author's permission.

Because authors couldn't trust the sales numbers even if their publishers had provided them, contracts were for a fixed fee rather than per-copy royalty payments. And if, as Goethe asserted, authors were in the dark as to their own value, it was in large part because publishers had every incentive to keep it that way. Goethe's proposal was a brilliant ploy that, Moldovanu and Tietzel argue, would compel Vieweg to tip his hand on what he thought a Goethe title was worth.

What makes Goethe's proposal like a Vickrey auction? Suppose that Veiweg figures he can earn 2,000 talers from *Hermann and Dorothea* (so that's his walk-away price). By exactly the same reasoning that would compel John Henry to bid $60 million in a Vickrey auction for the right to negotiate Matsuzaka's contract, Vieweg should bid exactly 2,000 talers—his full value—for the poem. Offering more than 2,000 only makes a difference if Goethe's sealed reserve is above 2,000—exactly the cases where Vieweg would rather pass. Similarly, offering less than 2,000 only affects the outcome if Vieweg's bid is *under* the reserve, in which case Vieweg misses out on acquiring a title worth 2,000 for something less than that amount.

Goethe certainly had some sense of what his particular genius was worth; the sealed "reserve price" he provided to his agent was 1,000 talers, about three or four times what even a popular author at the time could expect to receive for a work of that length. (By comparison, a day laborer in 1800 earned a wage of about a sixth of a taler per day.)

Why didn't Goethe just make a take-it-or-leave-it offer of 1,000 talers, a seemingly more straightforward approach? An ultimatum of that sort would generate exactly the same fee for Goethe—1,000 talers, if Vieweg's valuation was above that amount—while the "negotiation would be broken" if Vieweg's valuation was lower, just as with the sealed reserve.

But the response to take-it-or-leave-it is either yes or no. All it reveals to Goethe is whether his poems are worth more than 1,000 or less, but not how *much* more. Further, by revealing his walk-away price of 1,000 talers, Goethe was unnecessarily handing information to Vieweg that might be used against him in future negotiations. (Recall that Goethe told the publisher that if "his offer is lower than my demand, then I take my note back, unopened.")

Goethe surely realized that his best work was still ahead of him (including his most enduring work, *Faust*, the first part of which was published in 1808) and was already thinking ahead to future negotiations. Anticipating the new economics of the mid-twentieth century, he realized that where markets are concerned, information is power.

Vickrey Auction Markets for Everything

Although poets and stamp dealers may have intuited the value of second-price auctions, Vickrey provided the theoretical underpinning for these hunches, allowing the theory to be enriched and applied with greater sophistication. This in turn vastly expanded their audience. The Vickrey auction held enormous appeal not just to economists, who were captivated by its theoretical properties, but also those with more commercial interests. This was in part for the kinds of sales that interested Vickrey—auctioning off government-owned oil concessions or assigning road-building contracts—but also, with the advent of the internet, it extended to just about anything.

Vickrey's 1961 paper, along with refinements supplied by Edward Clarke and Theodore Groves in the early '70s, provided a sealed-bid mechanism that could easily be extended to work for more than one item. That meant its applications weren't limited to unique items like epic poems or baseball superstars; it could, in theory, be used by a milk-marketing board to sell off its members' output (this was the type of application Vickrey envisioned), or to auction Treasury bills to Goldman Sachs and J.P. Morgan. In what's called a multiunit Vickrey auction, the task facing bidders remains much the same, but instead of providing a single number in their sealed envelopes, prospective buyers would list a bid schedule providing a separate figure for what they'd be willing to pay, depending on how many units they receive. Suppose, for example, you're buying wholesale milk for a grocery chain. Maybe you'd pay $10,000 for the first ton of milk. That may be enough to supply your stores with the bare minimum they need, so you're only willing to pay a little less, say $9,000, for the second ton. If you're unlikely to sell much more than two tons in a week at the going price, you might not be willing to pay any more than $2,000 for a third ton. "Demand schedules" of this sort would be fed into the Vickrey-Clarke-Groves algorithm, and moments later you would find out how many tons of milk you'd bought, along with a bill for what you owed the marketing board.

In a brick-and-mortar age, the practical limitations in selling, say, Xbox 360s and flat-screen TVs via Vickrey auction are immediately evident. Imagine if, on a visit to Walmart, instead of reading off price tags you had a stack of envelopes to put in bids on a game console here, a TV there. Having expressed your willingness to pay for each item (or possibly your willingness to pay for a few of them), you'd return later in the day to see whether you were the new owner of a flat-screen TV or a new Xbox, or neither, or both. The logistical hurdles are overwhelming—the collating of pen-and-paper bids, the trips back and forth to the store, and so forth.

But the internet, by eliminating the need for sealed envelopes and physically visiting the store, had the potential to change all that. It wouldn't do away with the problem of interdependent demand, though. You might, for example, *only* want a new TV if you also got an Xbox, and only want the thirty-inch TV if you *don't* get the forty-inch one.[8] But maybe that wouldn't matter so much anyway: instead of having to make a special trip to the mall to put in your pen-and-paper bids, you could simply enter an online bid for one TV, see what happens, then try for another. It wouldn't be overly time consuming or cumbersome, as you need never check back or alter your bid.

This is, in fact, the way it works for eBay auction listings today. Much as stamp collectors mailed in proxy bids to dealer William P. Brown's New York auction house, you go to the web page for an item you'd like to bid on, enter your walk-away price, and forget about it till the auction ends. eBay takes care of raising your bid as necessary, and by Vickrey's reasoning, you can be sure that if the value you placed on the item is high enough, you'll get it.

The internet promised not just a more efficient way of selling but a new model of commerce where the economy would effectively become one big Vickrey auction with bidders remotely entering their willingness to pay for whatever they found on eBay or any one of the competing sites that were springing up around the internet. It's what led *The Economist* to write in 2000 that the internet introduced "the possibility of a permanent worldwide bazaar in which no prices are ever fixed for long, all information is instantly available, and buyers and sellers spend their lives haggling to try to get the best deals." (The Stanford economist Robert Hall was less sanguine—or maybe we should say less hysterical—in the role he thought auctions and dynamic pricing would play in the internet era. In his 2001 book *Digital Dealing*, he predicted—with reasonable accuracy, it turns out—that "auctions will predominate for collectibles, surplus equipment, industrial commodities, many securities, and sports and airline tickets.")[9]

Auctions weren't meant to be the only part of this internet bazaar, but they promised to be a big player in it. Pierre Omidyar's eBay was the first major online auctioneer, but the whiff of potential profits soon brought competition from other pioneers like Yahoo and Amazon.

Yet the promise of an internet auction takeover has long since fizzled. Amazon's auction site never took off, while Yahoo shuttered its auction business by 2007.

It's true that you can still register a proxy bid for any one of the millions of auctions listed on eBay today, but while the company is still known to many as an online auctioneer, by the end of 2012 less than 15 percent of listings used an auction format, down from nearly 100 percent just ten years earlier. The rest are plain-vanilla fixed-price sales, just as one would see listed from a third-party seller on Amazon, which makes buying things on eBay fundamentally not that different from the way people have done their shopping for the past century or so.

Given the critical importance of this shift in online commerce for eBay's bottom line, it's no surprise that data scientists within the company's research group have thoroughly studied the change. In a collaboration with Stanford economists, eBay researchers have dug into the reasons behind the decline of the company's auction business. Their findings matter to eBay executives mapping out business's future, and also for those of us who are simply trying to make sense of how the internet has changed the nature of markets and, just as important, the ways in which it hasn't.

If sellers aren't posting as many items for bid in an auction format as they used to, it could be because internet commerce (eBay included) has shifted from unique items like Pez collectibles, where there's a lot of uncertainty over what something is worth, to more pedestrian items like electronics equipment or groceries. It turns out that isn't the case, though: the shares of eBay's business across categories have remained steady despite the decline in auctions. So why the shift in selling format?

There's an old economics joke that goes something like this: if you strip a parrot of its colorful plumes and teach it to say "supply and demand" over and over and over again, you will have yourself a fine economist. It's funny because, well, it's partly true. In understanding what lies behind the decline of online auctions, it helps to see things from the perspective of each side the market.

Sellers might have realized that auctions are a costly hassle, or buyers might have decided they don't want to deal with auction-listed items. In either case, there won't be as many auctions.

Many economists spend their days trying to distinguish between supply- and demand-driven market phenomena: if the price of oil goes up, is it because people want to drive their cars more, or because OPEC is pumping out less oil than expected? If wages go down, is it because companies have cut their hiring demands, or because more people are looking for jobs? (Usually it's a bit of both.)

It turns out that eBay provides market researchers a near-perfect laboratory for making this distinction. Sellers run experiments to see how sensitive buyers are to higher prices, such as whether they pay more if extra photos are posted, and when eBay offered the chance to sell using fixed prices, sellers experimented with that as well to see what worked better, auctions or fixed prices.[10]

To get a feel for the researchers' approach, consider the following example. As we sit here this morning, we have an eBay window open, with a search for "new fifth generation iPod touch with 16 gigabytes of memory." The results show 122 listings. Amid the various colors, shipping options, and descriptions were more than just a few listed precisely as "Apple iPod touch 5th Generation Black & Silver (16 GB) (Latest Model)." Nearly 80 percent of these were available for fixed prices and the rest via auction.

The fixed-price listings were mostly in the $180 to $220 range (though one rather optimistic merchant listed one for $319.99). The prices of auctions-in-progress were lower, not surprisingly: among those that had received at least one bid, the prices ranged from $71.50 to $178.50, though at least one edged its way upward even in the half hour or so we spent on the site. (There is always a lot of action in the last few minutes of an auction. Proxy bids were meant to spare shoppers the trouble of tuning in through the flurry of activity that takes place as an auction closes, but it hasn't really worked out that way.[11])

Among this set of near-identical listings, compare, say, the sale of a buy-it-now-for-$200 iPod to an auction listing that ultimately goes for $180. If the researchers have done their job right in matching otherwise identical listings, the 10 percent discount on the auction listing is telling us something about how customers value the convenience of dealing with fixed price rather than auction sales, even when the latter are offered with the convenience of Vickrey-style proxy bids.[12] No matter how much you simplify a Vickrey auction, it still carries an inherent anxiety and nuisance of entering bids on items.

It turns out that the fixed-price premium on this day for iPods was no fluke. Auction prices are lower than fixed-price ones, and the gap has been widening in the years since *The Economist* prophesied that the internet would become a worldwide bazaar of haggling buyers and sellers. The "auction discount" was 3 percent in 2003; today it's stabilized at close to 15 percent.

The Economist's initial prediction was telling in its explanation that we would "spend our lives" haggling for the best deals. For a while that seemed like fun. The search for eBay "bargains" was a form of early internet entertainment: the thrill and suspense of competition and the occasional triumph. For most people, shopping on the internet these days is about as exciting as walking the detergent aisles at Walmart.

And part of why it's become so mundane is that for most things—like 16 GB iPods—there's just not that much uncertainty as to what they're worth. This morning, there's an endless supply available on Amazon for, you guessed it, around $190 or $200 dollars (shipping included).

If iPods are selling at a discount, why are there any being auctioned off on eBay at all? You might just as well ask why there are coupons for a dollar off a gallon of milk at the supermarket. Coupon clippers are so sensitive to prices (and value their time sufficiently little) that they spend their days poring over newspaper inserts in search of grocery bargains and, unlike busier or wealthier customers, will buy less milk or cereal unless they find a good deal. Coupons allow retailers to give cheapskate-specific discounts, while leaving prices high for other customers. Low-price auctions similarly serve to give time-rich, cash-poor customers a chance at getting 15 percent off their Black and Silver 16 GB iPod, while keeping prices high for everyone else.

The Problems with Vickrey Auctions

Vickrey probably wouldn't have been troubled by the fact that online shoppers don't care much for his auction; he was, after all, far more interested in allocation decisions of larger social consequence. But his design also sees scarce application in areas like government procurement, which had been Vickrey's primary motivation for building something better than a first-price auction in the first place. Nor has the Vickrey auction seen much action in the sale of state assets, where it matters not just how much revenue is generated but also that the asset—whether an oil concession or wireless spectrum—goes to the bidder who values it the most (because, it is presumed, he will make the most productive use of it).

This lack of use of the Vickrey auction was something of a puzzle to economists who were captivated by the way that, in its elegant simplicity, the mechanism helped magically cure the bidders' headaches over strategizing and overpaying.

It turned out that its simplicity wasn't up to dealing with the messy complications of most real-life auction situations. The second-price sealed-bid approach represented the best of all possible auction designs under the conditions laid out in Vickrey's 1961 paper, but its many shortcomings under more general conditions were laid bare in a 2006 essay by auction theorists Larry Ausubel and Paul Milgrom. In Ausubel and Milgrom's words, despite its "theoretical virtues, [the Vickrey auction] also suffers from weaknesses that are often decisive."[13]

For instance, there was no collusion in Vickrey's model and no shill bidding from buyers using multiple identities—strategies familiar to government contractors since time immemorial. Auction theorists figured out that, in sales involving more than a single item, the Vickrey mechanism made it even easier for bidders to benefit from preauction backroom meetings.[14] And although the seller would make out OK on average, it was entirely possible that under some conditions, a valuable government asset could change hands for a price of exactly zero. Imagine explaining to voters in a Senate hearing why your brilliant auction innovation had the net effect of transferring government property to Exxon or T-Mobile for free.

And that was just the start. The following year, an article in the academic journal *Operations Research*, "Thirteen Reasons Why the Vickrey-Clarke-Groves Process Is Not Practical," extended the list of problems. These weren't abstract considerations: when the New Zealand government sold its wireless spectrum via a series of Vickrey auctions in 1993, in one case a bidder offering $100,000 got the license for the second highest bid of just $6.[15]

And what of the MLB posting system that was in such desperate need of an overhaul in 2013? It would have seemed a perfect candidate for Vickrey's system: a single item for bid where first-price auctions had fared poorly because of uncertainty over what to offer, and the potential for career-destroying bids from unlucky auction "winners" who guessed wrong.

That was exactly what Morgan Sword, director of labor economics at MLB, thought after reading the *Wikipedia* entry for "Vickrey auction" as he looked into alternatives for the upcoming sale of Japanese star Masahiro Tanaka's contract. Tanaka, a pitcher on the Rakutan Golden Eagle roster, was expected to announce his interest in moving to the majors in November.

Sword's experiences in pitching the Vickrey auction to the various interested parties—teams in America and Japan, along with their players' unions—serve as a case study in the challenges in taking an idea from auction theory and putting it into practice.

The frailties of human nature never made it onto Rothkropf's list of Vickrey auctions' thirteen fatal flaws, but they proved critical to understanding the ultimate outcome of Sword's proposal to sell Tanaka's contract via a second-price auction. A crucial disadvantage of a first-price sealed-bid auction—the kind used to get Matsuzaka to Boston—was that an overbidding manager would find himself pilloried in the local press and possibly unemployed. But the Vickrey auction turned this problem on its head, offering the winner an easy excuse. By definition, no one overpays relative to the runner-up (because the winner pays the runner-up's bid).

This led to worries among team owners that, in the emotional atmosphere that characterized high-stakes player contracts, there would be so much upward pressure on bidding that they'd end up paying even more than under the old system. MLB owners rejected a standard English auction for much the same reason. Get a bunch of hypercompetitive owners and their associates in a room together, and bidding would surely get out of control—as they so often do. That's one reason why sellers use English auctions in the first place—to foster a sense of excitement that leads to competitive bidding and, the seller hopes, overpayment.

Sword suggested instead a hybrid of first- and second-bid auctions, where the winner paid an average of the top two bids, a proposal that eventually made its way to team owners to consider. He thinks they might have accepted it but for another peculiarity to the posting system. Major League teams face a payroll limit above which they're forced to pay a luxury tax. Major market teams like the Boston Red Sox and the New York Yankees regularly exceed the cap and have paid out hundreds of millions in taxes over the years, which went straight into the pockets of poorer franchises. The posting fees didn't count as salary, so other teams saw the $50 million payment the Red Sox made to the Seibu Lions as essentially a dodge of the salary cap. If the Sox had used those millions to pay more to Matsuzaka, it would've left them less wiggle room under the cap before facing luxury taxes.

What eventually came off the drawing board from Sword and his colleagues was an outright cap on posting fees of $20 million. The top three bidders in the auction would all have the right to negotiate with a player for his contract, a provision that Japanese players—who hoped to avoid getting sent to backwaters lacking big city amenities or sizeable Japanese communities—had long pushed for. The players association was happy enough to limit posting fees: it meant less of the transaction's proceeds would go to Japanese teams, and more would go to its members. American teams were at peace with it, particularly the ones in smaller markets.

So in the end, it was the Japanese teams who got screwed; the $50 million posting fee was now a thing of the past. But there was little they could do about it. Rakutan's total payroll added up to less than $50 million, and the team didn't generate enough profits to warrant turning down a $20 million check to keep their star in Japan. As Sword's boss put it, "We played last season without Tanaka, and we'll play the next one without him if we have to"—and anyway, $20 million was already well above what they thought they could get away with in buying off any team in Japan.

In the end Vickrey's undoing in the major league was the idiosyncrasies and specifics of the posting system and the incentives of the various parties involved. Complicated realities once again got in the way of the pristine elegance of Vickrey's design. It turns out that not everything is as easy to optimize as a roller-skating route through Harlem.

Things didn't end well for Goethe and his second-bid auction either. His agent, Herr Böttiger, sent a note to Vieweg, the publisher, ahead of the sale, which read as follows: "Now, tell me what can and will you pay? I put myself in your place, dear Vieweg, and feel what a spectator, who is your friend, can feel. Given what I approximately know about Goethe's fees from Göschen, Bertuch, Cotta and Unger, let me just add one thing: you cannot bid under [1,000 talers]." One thousand talers was exactly the figure Goethe had inscribed in his sealed envelope. Based on Vieweg's now-public sales records, *Hermann and Dorothea* went on to be a best seller, earning tens of thousands of talers for Vieweg and nary a penny more for poor Goethe. You can have the best-designed mechanism, but it doesn't do you the least bit of good if the process is corrupted.

It would be a mistake, however, to dismiss Vickrey's innovations based on their conspicuous absence from today's auction markets. It's like saying that Isaac Newton's contributions to physics were pointless because he never anticipated the theory of relativity. First, just as Newton's physics prove to be good enough for a range of circumstances, there are enormously important markets where variants on Vickrey's original design exist today. Most notable among these is Google's system for selling off search ads, AdWords, which instructs prospective advertisers to bid "the maximum amount you're willing to pay for each click on your ad (though the final amount you're charged per click—your actual CPC—could end up being less)." The reason buyers would be well-advised to do so is because AdWords is essentially a Vickrey auction.

And anyway, if Vickrey's exact mechanism hasn't aged well, his broader principles have: auction design is now a field unto itself within economics and sees widespread use in practice. If we don't delve into its many applications here, it's because one thing auction designers have learned is that every auction scenario—and hence the auction designed to meet its needs—is complicated in its own way.[16]

But the designers of auctions in some sense invoke Vickrey's pioneering efforts when they start by thinking about how, given the incentives of prospective bidders, an auction can best accomplish whatever a seller's objective may be, whether the seller is a revenue-maximizing vendor on eBay, a government aiming to ensure efficient exploitation of a resource, or, as Goethe endeavored, a producer or artist learning what his or her wares are worth.

It's important to appreciate how big a break this represents from how things used to be done, when there was a standard toolkit that sellers, whether private or public, used to unload their goods. And within the narrow set of options available, it's not even clear how much thought went into the decision of whether to use, say, a lottery or an English auction.

One oft-cited example of auction theory's triumph is the wireless spectrum auction of 1995. Previously, the Federal Communications Commission *had* in fact relied on a lottery: you applied for a cellular license in a particular locale, and if your number came up, you were the proud owner of spectrum somewhere in America. This might have been fair, since everyone had the same shot at getting each license, but it didn't generate much revenue for the government. Nor was it efficient, since it was generally more profitable to own licenses that were clustered geographically. The lottery might leave a spectrum owner with licenses in, say, Albuquerque and Albany, and he'd then have to find some way of swapping his Albany license for one in Santa Fe. (It also created a boon for Washington law firms that created "phone companies" for the sole purpose of bidding on licenses.[17])

When the FCC opened up the process to proposals from auction theorists, the resulting spectrum auction in 1995 involved a book-length set of rules describing the various contingencies and stipulations of participating in the spectrum sale. But the complications generated a big payday for Uncle Sam. The auction mechanism that Stanford economists Paul Milgrom and Robert Wilson proposed generated revenues of more than $7 billion.

The end result was a richer government and a more efficient world. If Vickrey was observing the auction from up above, he would surely have approved.

6

THE ECONOMICS OF PLATFORMS

IS THAT A MARKET IN YOUR POCKET
OR ARE YOU JUST HAPPY TO SEE ME?

In the year 1299, a merchant from the northern Italian city of Prato, renowned for its textiles, issued a formal complaint to the judges (known as wardens) in the County of Champagne.[1] The county, located in what is now northern France, near the border with Belgium and Luxembourg, was at the time independent of the French crown. Since around 1180, the region had hosted a series of trade fairs that drew merchants and financiers from all over Europe. It was, as one historian put it, "the fulcrum of European trade."[2]

The fairs—really, one continuous year-round affair—moved between six Champagne towns over the course of the year and stuck to a fixed six-week-long schedule in each town. A fair began with an entrée period of eight days during which merchants set up, followed by the days allotted for the cloth fair, the leather fair, and the sale of spices and other goods sold by weight (avoirdupois). In the last four days, accounts were settled. Inevitably, other trade sprung up around the fairs, catering to large groups of well-moneyed men. The taverns and brothels did a brisk business, as did other local business owners.

The merchant of Prato claimed one particular Florentine customer had not paid his bill by the fair's end. Instead, he had fled to London owing our friend from Prato 1,600 *livres tournois* (known in English as pounds).

Now, this is a lot of money. In fact, a business- and life-destroying sum by the standards of the time. Consider: there are around 360 pennies to a pound, and a craftsman in England could earn 4 to 5 pennies per day, or around 4 pounds a year. So 1,600 pounds is four hundred years' income for a skilled craftsman. In commodity terms, 1,600 pounds could buy you one hundred thousand capons or rabbits, many tons of salt or pepper, or twenty warhorses. You could rent all of the shops on London Bridge for ten years. You could pay the dowry for a baron's daughter, put on the wedding feast for four-teen hundred guests, and have enough left over to build six stone houses with courtyards. You could cover the annual income for an earl or duke.[3]

Our friend from Prato was not pleased and possibly broke.

The wardens of the fairs—a group of men empowered by the count of Champagne to administer the fairs and oversee judicial matters—sent a series of letters to the Florentine merchant and then, when he failed to respond, contacted the lord mayor of London.

The lord mayor, in turn, conducted an inquiry and determined that no debt was owed. If the inquiry was conducted in the manner of many a medieval proceeding, the Florentine paid off some functionary in the mayor's office and thought he had put the matter to rest.

He was mistaken: when the lord mayor informed the wardens that they were wrong, the Florentine merchant was in the clear, and that was that, the fair wardens responded by threatening a ban on all mercantile activities—not on the Florentine merchant, and not on other merchants from Florence, but on all merchants from London. At the same time, the wardens informed the London merchants of their ultimatum.

By the next year's fair (a blink of an eye in the time scale of medieval justice), the Florentine had paid the 1,600 *livres tournois* in full—at the insistence of the lord mayor, encouraged no doubt by the merchants of London.[4]

That the wardens held such sway in the courts of England over so great a distance speaks to the powerful role of the Champagne fairs in medieval commerce and to the efforts of the count of Champagne to keep it that way.

Fundamentalists of free-market economics think of economic exchange as springing up spontaneously, filling up the interstices of the economy wherever people see an opportunity to trade, as with the trading of Red Cross shipments in a World War II POW camp. In reality, like most social institutions, markets need love and attention to thrive. The count intuited the central role he played as a market maker: inviting the right sorts of participants (and more importantly, keeping the wrong sorts away), setting the rules, and punishing transgressors. In return, he got a little piece of each transaction, building his wealth enormously.

When the market maker's role is of particular importance for getting a market started and keeping it running, we call the market a *platform*. Credit cards, Facebook, your iPhone are all, each in its own way, carefully tended marketplaces that bring together various groups to transact: Visa cardholders and retail merchants, Facebook advertisers and the social network's members, iOS app designers and iPhone users.

The count of Champagne was, in his medieval way, a pioneer in market design. And the curious story of the merchant of Prato, his delinquent customer, and the count's response illustrates some of the principles that make a market platform tick.

As economists have focused their modeling efforts ever more on real world phenomena, leading researchers have turned their attention to platforms, bringing some much-needed clarity to the rules that dictate how these multisided markets work. As a result, we now have a deeper understanding of what makes a platform work and a set of guiding principles—many of which can be traced back to twelfth-century innovations in market design—that can help us build them better. Since platforms now encompass such significant parts of our lives, it's important to understand the trade-offs that come with participating in them.

The Economics of Platforms

It's not exactly clear when and why people started referring to economic phenomena like medieval fairs, credit cards, and internet services as platform markets. Some economists, ourselves included, find it needlessly confusing, given the multiplicity of ways that "platform" can be defined. Some are vaguely related to platform markets, others not. There are computing platforms, such as the Windows operating system that serves as a platform where other programs run, or the basic hardware on which the computer runs (as in Intel platform); political platforms, where candidates make grand proclamations about what they'll do once elected; and information platforms to spread one's brand, be it corporate, religious, or personal. It gets even more confusing when you consider that investors refer to platform businesses as companies that serve as springboards to building a larger presence in an industry (as in, "let's buy Intel as the first step in our global domination of the microprocessor business [cue evil laughter]").

Economists instead talk about two-sided markets or, as the case may be, multisided markets. You might reasonably ask what market doesn't have two sides. You go to the supermarket, go job hunting, or hire a contractor to renovate your kitchen. These are market transactions with buyers and sellers: two sides and a set of market prices that, economic theory holds, makes the world a better, or at least more efficient, place.

A supermarket (or any store, really) is actually a one-sided market in that, to a certain extent, it need only deal with one set of customers at a time. It buys the groceries to stock its shelves, with its purchasing managers making sure there's enough variety to satisfy shoppers' wants and needs. Rarely do a grocery store's suppliers meet the shoppers, unless you happen to run into the guy stocking the bread on a quiet afternoon.

But lots of markets involve more direct contact among their participants. These true multisided markets require an extra push to get off the ground and constant nurturing to reach their potential. The person who provides this extra push, the market maker, creates the platform where two or more customers meet and designs it in such a way that both sides want to show up and, when they do, walk away satisfied with their transactions. Amazon and eBay serve this market-making role for buyers and sellers of just about everything; Angie's List does it for plumbers, electricians, and other contractors on one side and those looking to fix or renovate their homes on the other. There need not be only two sides: Google's Android is a meeting point for makers of smart phones like LG and

THE ECONOMICS OF PLATFORMS | 109

Samsung, app designers, and consumers. The business networking service LinkedIn similarly brings together corporate recruiters, job hunters or employees, and advertisers. The list goes on, including some of the recent "sharing economy" companies that have gotten so much attention: Uber, Lyft, Airbnb, Postmates, and many other online marketplaces.

The market maker faces a delicate balancing act in satisfying the needs and wants of each side. And indeed a platform isn't much good unless all sides agree to participate. Just as no one would visit a supermarket that stocked only a limited supply of cornflakes, eBay wouldn't get many visitors if the only items for bid were a couple of old Pez dispensers. Nor would anyone bother to post their surplus Beanie Babies if they didn't expect it to be seen by a reasonable volume of potential customers. The participants on each side of the market are of the chicken-and-egg variety.

This is less of a problem for a one-sided market like a grocery store, which often buys its inventory from manufacturers before putting it up for sale. A farmer doesn't care how many shoppers are in the aisles, since he's already sold his potatoes to the store.[5] But on a platform, neither side will come unless the market maker actively nudges the process along. The market maker's job is to attract participants—to get the right people (and enough of them) to show up. In fact, on a platform, the value for one side grows as more people show up on the other.

eBay's job doesn't end when it's convinced sufficient numbers of buyers and sellers to visit the site. If a fair number of transactions on its platform end in acrimony, neither side will stick around for very long. So a platform also needs to set the rules and resolve disputes to ensure that doesn't happen. The rules of the platform matter.

As a working definition, then, we'll say a platform is a market where two groups (often buyers and sellers) interact via a go-between who makes sure that participants are happier (and the market more efficient) than they'd be if left to be guided only by the invisible hand. If you think this seems like an overly broad definition, platforms expert and Boston University economist Marc Rysman would agree. What market wouldn't benefit from someone or something sitting in the middle of transactions to make them more reliable and transparent? Two-sidedness is more a matter of degree. For some platforms, it's critical that there be an intermediary that tinkers with prices and other inducements to ensure that there are balanced numbers on each side: a dating platform aimed at hetero men with no women would quickly unravel, as would a retail platform with few sellers or overly narrow product offerings. And some market transactions require stronger-handed referees than others. It's no big deal if you order batteries on the internet and they aren't quite what you'd hoped for; but an internet nanny service needs to make sure there aren't any "defective" sellers offering their services.[6]

Really, any exchange can be set up as a platform, or structured more like a traditional one-sided market. The count of Champagne could have bought from traveling leather-goods vendors and then retailed the products himself. Apple could similarly produce or buy all the apps it offers to customers rather than intermediating between phone users and programmers. And Amazon does both: it buys and resells some kinds of items, while serving as a platform intermediary for others, in whatever combination will make it the most money. If becoming a platform is a choice, these days it's a popular one among entrepreneurs and the venture capitalists that fund them. Why? What's in it for the platform builder, the market maker?

If you think of a platform as a playing field, the owner is selling tickets to any player who wants to get onto the field, no matter which side he or she is playing on, or how many teammates have already joined. A company running a platform probably doesn't care which team wins (in the sense of one side, or player, benefiting the most from the platform). It just wants to sell tickets to a lot of players and make sure the game is played on its turf.[7] To do so, you have to ensure that the players you let onto the field actually enhance the platform's value, so both sides stick around to play. (Think about the value proposition at eBay if conmen dominated its sellers' ranks.)

Looking at a two-sided market through this lens—as a space where people meet and not just where trade takes place—is a new angle to understanding exchange. The difference between one-sided and two-sided markets is subtle but meaningful. It changes the way that we might approach the market as a business or a consumer. And it affects how a regulator decides whether a platform can govern itself, or if there's a need to step in to impose some rules on the businesses using the platform.

The seemingly obscure rules of platforms have a great effect in your life. As we've noted, platforms are ubiquitous—video game consoles, container shipping, credit cards, package delivery, magazine and newspaper businesses, web search, real estate brokerage, HMOs, shopping malls, stock exchanges, to name a few. And they're seemingly becoming more common with each passing day, mediating more and more of our experiences. And no wonder: it's easier to set up a meeting place now that we no longer need to convene en masse at events like the Champagne fairs. We can just log on and meet in cyberspace instead. And so, we now find dates, book travel, buy groceries, send instant messages, and hail taxis—all via online platforms. More recently, the much-vaunted internet of things is bringing us yet another generation of platform business models, some amazing, some terrifying, and some, like internet-enabled cars, a bit of both. As cars move from being internal combustion engines with wheels to software platforms that are connected to the internet and to one another, we can imagine all sorts of potential for them, some of which will make our lives better (fewer accidents with autonomous cars and more apps that plug into them) and some of which will make us even more vulnerable (long-distance software hacks). But regardless, they'll be governed by the same rules that make other platforms tick.

Currently, entrepreneurs and venture capitalists—spurred by the success of Facebook, LinkedIn, Uber, and many others—are pouring money into new platform businesses. But not every market is suited to a platform model. Lots of start-ups that now enjoy lavish funding and media attention will have people looking back, shaking their heads, trying to figure out what they were thinking back in 2016. If there isn't a problem with buyers and sellers already finding one another or some other reason for a market to fail (or never form), then there isn't much call for a platform in the first place. If you build it, there's a good chance no one will come.

In 2014, *New York* magazine reported on the emerging competition among laundry service platforms ("Let's, Like, Demolish Laundry"). It's not clear what market failure they're solving. Dry cleaners already deliver; they're providing the undifferentiated commodity of clothes cleaning, where it'll be exceedingly obvious after the first pickup and delivery whether they're doing their job. Maybe the internet will make this process a bit more efficient, but a platform business it ain't. It's an example of what our friend and MIT strategy professor Pierre Azoulay calls "the internet of what my mom won't do for me anymore." Sure, in a few years you'll still be able to go online and find someone to wash your clothes for you. But whoever takes the job probably won't be profiting that much from the privilege of doing so.

Contrast that with the classic lemons market—the market for used cars. As with laundry, there's a race to see who will be the used car dealer of choice for the internet age. If one of them comes up with a way of making the lemons market work, they'll be richly rewarded for it.

While every multisided market has its own eccentricities, there are some overarching principles like these, which can help to clarify where two-sided markets are most needed, and why they take the particular forms they do.

The Variety of Rules

Market makers are confronted with many choices in the rules they choose for their platforms, which decide who shows up and how they interact. Different rules yield different crowds and different transactions.

It's for this reason that credit cards are the canonical example of a two-sided platform: credit card companies all started with the same basic objective of connecting retailers and shoppers via a line of credit but ended up with very different ways of making this connection.[8]

Customers have long been able to buy goods on credit, but until the 1950s each customer had to manage a separate credit relationship with each store. You'd have a line of credit with the local pharmacy, another with the butcher, and yet another at Sears. It was convenient, up to a point: instead of paying cash for each purchase, you could sit down at the end of the month and pay the total bill by check. Husband and wife might share an account and keep tabs on what the family had purchased. Stores liked it, despite its risks, because it boosted customer loyalty.

Yet it was crazily inefficient, relative to just paying a single monthly bill. The market-making opportunity this created was well recognized by banks. By the late 1950s there had been maybe a dozen attempts to start a credit card with centralized billing.[9] All of these efforts failed: not enough stores signed on to make it worthwhile for customers to apply for cards, and not enough consumers got cards to convince stores to accept them.

The chicken-and-egg problem was, at that point, seemingly insurmountable.

In 1958, the grandiose ideas of a Bank of America executive named Joseph Williams solved the problem—albeit at great expense to the company, as it turned out. Williams chose Fresno, California, for his ambitious credit card launch. With its population of 250,000, 45 percent of whom were Bank of America customers, Fresno had the density of customers that gave the program at least a chance of taking off. Williams and his colleagues prepped the retailer side of the platform by all but promising merchants that they'd have a bunch of customers trying to use their new cards. And wouldn't it be a shame if they had to turn away the business? A good many Fresno retailers signed on to the offer, which, after all, was one it was dangerous to refuse.

Williams and his team followed up on the promise of making sure there would be customers with cards, mailing sixty thousand live cards (not one of those offers you get in the mail these days, actual working cards) to Bank of America customers, letting them know how the program worked. It probably felt a bit like an invitation to go out and spend someone else's money. And spend they did. Through a combination of aggressive marketing and arm twisting, Williams had finally launched the credit card business.

But Williams wasn't the only one pursuing this effort. Rumors had it that another bank was going to do a similar drop in San

Francisco, Bank of America's home city. Those competitive pressures forced Williams to move forward faster than was, at least in hindsight, prudent. The Fresno test seemed to be going well enough that Williams and his team expanded the program, using a similar approach in San Francisco, Sacramento, and Los Angeles. By October of 1959, the bank had mailed more than two million cards throughout California, and more than twenty thousand merchants had accepted the new BankAmericard.

The bank, meanwhile, made its money by sitting in between those two sides of the market, charging its customers interest and late fees and taking a piece of every transaction from the merchants.

For a while, the newly launched card appeared to be a great success, but there was a fatal flaw in the design of Williams's platform. We've kind of given it away already: today, to get a credit card you need to apply for one, and before you actually get your card and line of credit, the issuer takes a look at your credit score, salary, and other predictors of whether you'll ever pay off your balance. Not so in these early days. Williams's leap of faith in sending out cards to two million Californians, with perhaps a shaky understanding of their new credit lines, turned out to have been severely misplaced.

Williams had forecast a 4 percent delinquency rate. It was closer to 25 percent. And one wholly unanticipated result was the birth of credit card fraud, including widespread identity theft. Although Williams had understood that he needed to jump-start participation on both sides of the market, he violated another basic principle of platform design: he failed to attract the right *types* of customers as participants. If you're handing out credit cards, credit worthiness is critical, to say the least.

Williams left Bank of America in late 1959, having lost the bank somewhere between $9 million and $20 million (between $75 and $160 million in today's dollars). But the bank was able to salvage the program, which, after all, had an impressive (if flawed) installed base. The bank moved the program under the supervision of its loan department, which sorted through its existing cardholders, raising the credit available to some and cutting off others. In 1965 Bank of America began expanding the program beyond California to the rest of the United States through partnerships with other banks. (Interstate banking regulation prevented them from expanding nationally themselves.) And in the late 1960s, the program went international (the Barclaycard was the UK equivalent). Bank of America gave up control of the program in 1970, and in 1975 the network changed its name to Visa.

Williams had the insight that you needed to do *something* to make cards attractive to consumers. His approach of just issuing a card to anyone who asked for one (and, initially, even those who didn't) turned out to be toxic to his career, but there's more than one way to build a platform. Indeed, as illustrated by American Express, or Amex, which launched its card in 1957, and Sears's introduction of the Discover card in the mid-1980s, there can be wildly divergent, but equally successful, visions of how to jump-start a platform, even ones in the same industry. Both managed to get merchants and shoppers together and neither lost $20 million doing it.

American Express began as an express mail service in Buffalo, New York, in 1850. The company introduced money orders in 1882 and, inspired by the CEO's difficulty in getting ready cash during his European summer tour, introduced travelers' checks in 1891. The company quickly earned a reputation for taking care of its customers, built on its initial guarantee of getting packages across the country fast. That image morphed into a broader reputation for luxurious but practical customer care when the company's European outlets helped Americans stranded in Europe by the outbreak of World War I. People concerned with transcontinental express package delivery and having ready cash on hand when traveling internationally were, at the time, a rather exclusive and enviable customer base.

Amex launched its charge card business in 1957, with 250,000 accounts. The key to Amex-as-platform was its choice to use its exclusivity and high standards as the magnet that brought the two sides of its market together. In contrast to handing out cards to all comers for free, Amex charged six dollars to open each account (one dollar more than its closest competitor, Diners Club) and also charged merchants a steeper fee, which many were willing to pay to access Amex's higher net worth and more credit-worthy customers. On the other side of the equation, they offered incentives and services to their customers and, later, tiered services. Amex introduced the Gold Card in 1984 and then the Platinum (and other) cards, each with a higher annual fee (and more perks). Pulling out an Amex card was an instant source of status. Travelers' checks were for the masses, while the charge card was exclusive. But they both were built on a common platform of Amex-accepting merchants and their Amex-using customers.

Sears took the opposite tack in 1985 with its Discover card. Initially, Sears tried to leverage the fact that it was at the time the largest retailer in the country to attract customers by accepting only Discover cards in its stores. But that proved not to be enough to jump-start the card. So Sears started paying people to take their cards. Literally.

Discover carried no annual fee and offered cardholders a cash-back bonus, a novel idea at the time in which a percentage of the amount spent would be refunded to the account, depending on how much the card was used. Sears wooed other retailers (who might have been reluctant to support a Sears product) by offering significantly lower merchant fees than competing cards. The card took off, proving so popular that soon other credit card platforms were racing to put together similar offerings.

Bank of America, American Express, and Sears had set out to solve the same problem—creating a credit card platform that would unite a particular set of consumers on one side with a large number of retailers on the other. Yet they ended up with subtly different solutions to getting the two sides they wanted on board. The rules you choose in building a platform matter a great deal, but there are many paths to success.

Diversity in platform design shows up in lots of other industries. Some video game systems, for instance Nintendo, Sega, and Sony, charge developers a fixed fee together with a per-unit royalty for games they produce. But Microsoft, in an attempt to speed up the development of new offerings, does not charge fixed fees, only a royalty. Google and Apple have dueling platforms in the mobile market—Android versus iOS—that similarly compete for developers and users on each side of their platform apps.

Why do you care that you're an unwitting participant in e-business's many platform wars? It might help you choose more thoughtfully among the competition and appreciate the many elements that make a "good" platform. These lessons aren't obvious. As we'll see below, companies' fortunes have been wagered and lost based on misunderstandings of what makes a platform tick.

Platform Builder as Internet Cop

The economist who did the most to formalize our understanding of two-sided markets is Jean Tirole, a Frenchman who won the Nobel Prize in 2014.[10] Within economics, Tirole is known for his superhuman productivity and, relatedly, his incredible clarity of thought. According to one of his former students, Tirole writes his papers out by hand, to be typed out by his assistant. The drafts never include scratch work or deletions—the full arc of an argument is clear in his mind as he writes out his ideas. At the Toulouse School of Economics, where he has worked since 1996, graduate students joked that there must be a dozen little Jean Tiroles hidden in his basement writing the manuscripts, given the rate at which they appeared.

Tirole wrote the book, quite literally, on industrial organization, the field within economics that aims to understand why markets are organized as they actually appear—why some industries consist of two dominant players (like Coke and Pepsi), while others more closely resemble Kenneth Arrow's perfectly competitive ideal. You can only confront these questions if you consider the strategic choices companies like Microsoft or Coke might make to try to ensure they're the only game in town, and the regulatory decisions an enlightened government might choose to make sure they aren't. Tirole's *Theory of Industrial Organization* remains the standard reference on the topic, despite being published nearly three decades ago. (It also has more than thirteen thousand citations on Google Scholar, which is extremely unusual for a textbook; it's about twice as many citations as Paul Samuelson's classic *Economics* text, even though the latter is fifty years older.[11])

Tirole's Nobel is emblematic of the postwar trend in economics—begun by George Akerlof's market for lemons paper and continued by the many applied theorists that followed—toward tailoring models to circumstance. As a result, it's hard to boil his opus down to media-friendly sound bites. As he told Binyamin Appelbaum of the *New York Times* after his prize had been announced: "There's no easy line in summarizing my contribution and the contribution of my colleagues. . . . The way you regulate payment cards has nothing to do with the way that you regulate intellectual property or railroads. . . . It's not a one line thing."[12]

Tirole also embodies the increasing incursion of economic theory into the functioning of markets economists study as they find themselves advising Silicon Valley companies and designing government health-care exchanges and spectrum auctions. Despite his low profile, Tirole's advice is much sought after by the companies that are the object of his study: it's of immense value to businesspeople to talk with someone who can strip a complicated situation down to its bare essentials, whether expressed in algebra or prose. The dense mathematics of his academic papers has served as a basis for regulatory policies on telecommunication networks.

Tirole also applied himself to the question of how to regulate credit cards, which in turn led to a series of papers that aimed to understand two-sided markets more broadly: examining why they exist, what makes them different from the one-sided variety, and how competing platforms like Visa and Amex vie for customers on both sides of their respective markets, and providing some guiding principles for builders of two-sided markets and the authorities that regulate them.

Much of Tirole's work on platforms takes as its starting point that a two-sided market is one where participants on either side couldn't simply find one another and strike a bargain in the absence of the platform standing between them.[13] If they could, then they wouldn't need the services of the platform.

More often than not, the market maker, sitting in the middle of a market where the various sides have trouble agreeing, turns into a referee, mediator, guarantor, and sometime policeman. If the market maker does the job right, the two sides work together a lot more often and do so more efficiently than in his absence. The Champagne wardens ensured that the merchant of Prato got paid, other traders took notice, and the Champagne fairs thrived. Successful internet platforms, such as eBay, Uber, and Amazon, have similarly figured out ways of making most transactions run smoothly and acting as arbitrator in those that don't (and, in Uber's case, using a proprietary algorithm that governs how to connect drivers and customers).

The market maker can screen out undesirables from all sides of the platform, but as cases like eBay and Uber suggest, often the job is left to platform participants themselves. The platform manager makes customer feedback possible, and in theory, the wisdom of crowds takes care of the rest, solving the asymmetric information problem that George Akerlof identified as the enemy of market function back in 1970.

This has led to all sorts of match-making platforms for goods or services where it was hard to find a reliable provider in the pre–internet era.

If Akerlof had wanted to renovate his house in the '70s, for instance, he would have had to find a Berkeley-area contractor who had the skills for the job, had the time to take it on, was reliable, would quote a fair price, and wouldn't try to jack up the price once he'd knocked down a few walls. Plus, there were intangibles, things the customer would have a hard time writing a contract on or enforcing, like whether the contractor would track mud through the house or smoke near an open window. As a friend of ours says, if you have to refer back to the contract, something has probably already gone terribly wrong.

In this pre–internet era, you'd likely ask your friends and family for suggestions, but that'd usually generate a pretty narrow set of options. The Yellow Pages weren't much help, since they just listed available firms. An ad might indicate a successful business, one that generated sufficient revenues to pay for it, but that was a pretty weak signal. You might start at the top, but could you really trust AAAA Contracting services, just because their name happened to start with four A's?

As a result of the opacity of the market and the difficulty for the inexpert homeowner to even know what's going on once renovations began, home contractors have, traditionally, been a profession of decidedly ill repute. Everyone has a horror story, or at least could relate the horror stories of others. In case you don't, there's even a website called contractorsfromhell.com, with tales of woe running from useless plans to cost overruns to leaky pipes, spontaneously collapsing roofs, and all manner of shoddy workmanship. (One horror storyteller warns against ever hiring a contractor that advertises directly, in the same way you'd never want to call a lawyer who boasts in billboard and subway advertisements about the million-dollar payouts he's won or buy anything, money-back guarantee or not, from a late-night infomercial.)

That's where a two-sided platform like Angie's List—that ubiquitous advertiser on NPR—comes in, connecting homeowners in search of a contractor with the right person for the job.

Without claiming that Angie's List has turned home repair into a frictionless process, we can at least say that it's made it a whole lot better. Customers can comment on the contractors they've hired, which means that, even if you don't know anyone who's worked with a particular plumber, you at least have some indication of whether he knows what he's doing, how fast he works, and how accurate his estimates usually turn out to be. *And* you'll know whether he tracks mud in his customers' houses or smokes in their bathrooms, because Angie's List will tell you all that, for a fee. Essentially, once you find yourself outside the frictionless world of perfect markets, there's a potential role for an intermediary to sit between the two sides.[14]

Lots of market evangelists have taken the notion that better technology and more nuanced feedback algorithms will end the informational problems that were the focus of Akerlof, Spence, and other information economists. One article on the libertarian Cato Institute's website recently trumpeted in its title that we are approaching "The End of Asymmetric Information." We doubt it. They're confronting some pretty thorny information and enforcement challenges, and it's far from clear that the techno-utopians will win the day.

A wronged textile merchant from medieval times or a disgruntled homeowner from 1980 has nothing on the parental anxieties of the twenty-first century. This has led to enormous inefficiencies in the market for babysitters, with parents focused on a narrow set of sitter options: the neighbors' kids, a friend's sitter, or a bonded babysitting service. Would-be babysitting platforms like Urbansitter and Care.com argue that some combination of background checks, customer feedback, and social network connections will be sufficient to get you to leave your toddlers alone with a sitter or nanny you've never met. Would *you*?

Yes and no. As consumers of nanny platforms ourselves, we can attest that the wider set of options that immediately present themselves at log-in is overwhelming. A search as narrow as current Boston University students looking for after-class employment, living within one mile of a particular zip code, yields dozens of options and a ready summary of their formal qualifications. And the customer reviews? Where sitters even have them, they're not a big help. The process of calling references and conducting in-person interviews to gather soft information about whether you really trust this person remains largely unchanged from when we were first hiring sitters a dozen years ago.

Their imperfections notwithstanding, the advent of babysitter platforms is bad news for brick-and-mortar nanny placement services, whose businesses are surely suffering. But we're still skeptical that any intermediary, however diligent, will overcome the anxieties of the modern helicopter parent. We doubt that day will ever arrive. Asymmetric information is dead? Long live asymmetric information.

The Network Externalities of Ladies' Night

The calculation of how to set prices is a lot more complicated on platforms than in one-sided markets because they are defined by what economists call network externalities, where one person's purchase makes the item more valuable for other would-be consumers.[15] Obviously, this isn't the case for groceries: the happiness I get from a box of Oreos isn't affected by whether you prefer to spend your money on Oreos or chocolate-chip cookies or kale. But things are different for telephones: my phone is useless unless there's at least one other person who also has one, and as more phones are sold and the network of phone owners expands (and hence the more people I can call), my phone becomes ever more valuable. So each phone purchase generates value not just for the buyer but anyone else who already has one.

This has at least two implications for the way networked businesses are run. First, since the bigger a company gets, the more valuable it is to each successive customer, there's a huge premium on expanding your customer base. As a result, platforms may want to set prices lower than businesses that sell unnetworked products, like Oreos. To get the Discover card up to speed quickly, Sears charged no fee and even offered its customers cash back—which is quite odd, when you stop to think about it.

One of Tirole's platform insights—the one with the most tangible consequences for the person on the street—is that two-sided markets are in many ways just a particular case of network externalities, one that works across the two sides of the platform. And that leads to some extreme differences in how the two sides are treated, differences that would be totally mystifying without some appreciation of the basics of platform economics.

Why, for example, does Google let you search the web for free, even though maintaining its primacy in the search engine market costs the company a fortune in R&D, computing infrastructure, and courting users via advertising? The reason is, of course, because a bigger user base allows Google to extract ever-higher revenues from the other side of the market—the advertisers, who pay for search listings. In this case, stocking Google search results with more paid ads doesn't do much to enhance the customer experience, so there's a wide gap between what each side of the market pays to meet on Google.

This state of affairs is entirely common in the realm of two-sided markets: many credit card companies don't charge cardholders or even give them discounts, while merchants pay through the nose; shopping malls, a two-sided market from an earlier era, charge their tenants rent, while offering free parking and other inducements to attract shoppers.

Sometimes the way that platforms charge can look perverse, until you understand the logic. Shopping malls charge their larger stores *less* money than smaller businesses because without those anchors to draw shoppers, the mall couldn't exist. Or consider ladies' night at your local bar: the fact that ladies get in free is discriminatory. But bars have figured out that men put much greater value on being surrounded by lots of women than the other way around. Ladies' night is their way of ensuring there will be enough women at the bar to attract male customers who are happy to pay to get in. Writ large, you might think that this should be regulated (no discriminatory pricing!), but singles bars might have a tougher time surviving if they couldn't exploit this apparent pricing anomaly.

Some platforms have even performed the truly amazing trick of, as Harvard Business School professor Ben Edelman puts it, getting their *non*customers to pay them. How exactly does that work? You probably already did it a dozen times in the past week: any time you pay cash at an establishment that accepts credit cards, you're subsidizing the customers that use cards. This is because most retailers charge the same price for all transactions, regardless of whether they involve credit, debit, or cash, or whether the charge goes to a high-fee card like Amex or a lower-fee Visa, MasterCard, or Discover. The retailer might like to charge 3 percent more for high-commission card sales, but they don't; instead, they charge a "blended" price to all customers.[16]

Think credit card companies are the only ones? Think again. The internet has empowered dozens of intermediaries to pull the same stunt: OpenTable, the online reservation platform, gives cash rewards to diners, but they don't see an extra charge from restaurants. Expedia, the online travel booking platform, hands out reward points, but your flight costs the same whether you book through them or directly on an airline's website—the list goes on and on.

This might sound like a fantastic deal for you, the consumer— after all, airlines, restaurants, and stores are footing the bill, and you're reaping the benefits—until you stop to consider the fact that you might be happier carrying around a bit more cash and getting a 3 percent discount when you use it, rather than a 1 percent cash rebate from Visa. Professor Edelman, also a lawyer by training, has argued that this is one of the many places market makers might just have a little too much power over their platforms. Such practices make credit card issuers compete too much on offering rebates rather than reducing fees to retailers. It makes consumers worse off by taking away their choice of cash versus credit. Overall, Edelman argues, society would be better off if platforms would just stop strong-arming participants on one or more sides of the market. Credit card companies won't do it on their own. After all, if you can get paid by noncustomers, that's a fantastic gig. It's the job of government regulators to reign in the power of the all-powerful market maker in many two-sided markets.[17]

The credit card market also serves to indicate why the inequitable treatment of participants on different sides of the platform is so common. Although both sides of a credit card transaction need each other (your card is useless unless it's honored at many merchants; a card reader is a waste of money if shoppers don't use credit), the two sides wield differing degrees of market power in negotiating with the platforms that compete for their business. You can swipe any card on the same machine to make a purchase, so stores tend to honor any card a customer might choose. Stores are, in platform parlance, multihoming.

But customers tend to pick sides in platform competition. Many of us have more than one or two of the major credit cards in our wallets. But often we have one default choice that we use for most of our purchases. We are single-homing as credit card users.

If a two-sided market is only useful when *both* sides are on board, then there's intense rivalry to enlist the single-homers, who can shop around among competing options—different malls, a range of credit cards, and so forth—to pick the one that offers the best deal. And the multihomers? They'll sign on with everyone and—once platforms realize they don't need to work hard to attract them—pay the price for their platform promiscuity.

Platform Businesses for Everything

It's no wonder the business world is filled with platform envy. Platform owners, if they do their job right in picking the right area and setting up the rules, can make a lot of money just by existing. Once you've got your transaction generating and policing infrastructure up and running, with the network externalities all but forcing all market participants to meet on your site, you get to sit back and watch the money roll in. Uber takes a cut of every ride, Airbnb of each home stay, and Google all but prints money via its search ad business as long as it just maintains the quality of its internet search algorithm.

That helps explain why venture capitalists are throwing money at everything: dog walking, grocery buying, grocery delivery, used car purchases, new car purchases, clothes cleaning, house cleaning, house sitting.

But if everyone recognizes the awesomeness of owning a plat-form—as they seem to and then some—there's going to be some intense competition to see who emerges as the dominant format. That's why would-be platforms need their millions of dollars in ven-ture capital funding up front: in addition to product development, they often need to spend extravagantly on "buying" a customer base that serves as the foundation of a networked business. When it was just getting started, PayPal, for instance, gave new customers ten dollars just for signing up and more for recommendations.

No one knows this better than Sony who, having seen their Betamax format lose out to VHS in the 1980s, had a chance for a do-over in the market for high-definition digital video devices when the company's Blu-ray technology came up against Toshiba's HD DVD format in the 2000s. The formats were evenly matched on playback and recording quality. It was just a question of which com-pany would build up a big enough library of titles and sufficient user base to tip the balance in its favor, thus starting the virtuous (from the winner's perspective) cycles of ever-wider use and ever-greater presence of offerings.

Both sides spent lavishly to come out on top. Sony put its Blu-ray technology into its newly released PlayStation 3 video console, ensuring an enormous installed customer base. Toshiba countered by paying Microsoft to put HD DVD players into the Xbox 360 console, which competed head-on with PlayStation. While Block-buster threw its support behind Blu-ray (back in the days when the now-defunct company's support meant something), Toshiba report-edly paid movie studios Paramount and DreamWorks US $150 mil-lion in exchange for a commitment to release films only on HD DVD.

Both sides spent fortunes in a series of moves and countermoves. The scales tipped toward Blu-ray eventually, as studio after studio decided that, given the support already enjoyed by the format, it was no longer worthwhile to offer new releases on HD DVD. But any profits that Sony might have made from winning control of the DVD market had long since been spent in the fight for dominance.

Even worse, with their focus on the DVD wars, they took their eye off the larger technological shift—video streaming—that ended up killing the DVD business altogether. In fact, by the time Toshiba discontinued HD DVD production in early 2008, Amazon, TiVo, and Apple were already streaming movies, and Microsoft's Bill Gates had pronounced the outcome of the Blu-ray-HD DVD format war largely irrelevant because "[e]verything's going to be streamed. . . . So, in a way, it's not even clear how much this one counts."

Raise a Glass to Champagne

All of this can help us to understand the Champagne fairs as a platform rather than a one-sided market. Of course, the count didn't set out to design a platform, but instinctually, he basically did. And he did it well: the Champagne fairs thrived for nearly a century, largely thanks to the wise choices he made in medieval platform design.

The count's efforts weren't out of the goodness of his heart: the fairs provided Champagne's leaders with immense fortunes, which allowed them to sponsor crusades to the Holy Land and encourage the founding of the Order of the Knights Templars. They had enough time to engage in writing poetry and other courtly pursuits themselves even as they hosted some of the most renowned artists of the age.

The count intuitively knew how to make the fair-cum-platform work. He avoided selling privileges to special interest groups. Instead, he made generalized institutional guarantees to everyone. He established an impartial law and enforced it at multiple levels—even, as we've seen, by using other rulers, like the lord mayor of London. By 1170, he had established the fair wardens to police the fair and to witness the signing of contracts. He established four levels of courts within the fair to resolve disputes and to make sure contracts were enforced (the courts had the power to fine, confiscate, ban, and incarcerate).

The count also provided broad protection and security to fair participants. He founded the Hotel-Dieu for visiting merchants and erected fortifications around the fair location, which must have been a tempting target for brigands and more legitimate neighbors alike. The count's protection even extended to those traveling to the fair. As early as 1148, when a French nobleman robbed money changers traveling from Vezclay, the count wrote to the French crown insisting that the money changers be made whole. By 1220 such protection extended to Italy as well.

The count even guaranteed loans and gave some concessions on market dues to get other groups (like the church) involved—just like some credit cards pay their customers to attract their business and mall owners give discounts to anchor stores to attract more foot traffic. He also encouraged traders to settle all debts and credits by notary bill instead of cash, so that the merchants could travel without the burden of a great deal of money.

The count had a strong incentive not to show any favoritism and to make sure the rules were applied evenly—that's what made the fairs so attractive. This begat a virtuous circle of medieval commerce: knowing that the fairs would be around for the long haul, attendees worked hard to develop reputations for fair dealing, knowing they'd have repeated interactions with the same set of participants each year and that word of cheats and scoundrels would quickly spread. The rules the wise count established also helped make sure that all the necessary parties kept coming back once they first showed up.

These rules help explain why the merchants of London capitulated to the fair wardens' demands so quickly. Getting booted out of the fair would be the equivalent of being blacklisted from Amazon in a world where that was the only way of reaching your customers, which isn't that far from the circumstances businesses operate in today. Devastating. Their businesses would have collapsed.

But despite the count's getting the rules right, the fairs eventually did end, subject to too many outside forces and, perhaps, temptations. Wars, a failure to enforce the rules, a shortsighted French crown—all led to the platform's unraveling.

The counts lost control of Champagne when the king of France, who wasn't one to take the long view, began consolidating his power. The king was far more interested in extracting money from the merchants—and fast—than he was in continuing to invest in the long-term health of the fairs. For example, the king started selling special dispensations that allowed richer merchants to flout the rules of the fair (the equivalent of Amazon charging sellers for the right to cheat their customers). He also began showing favoritism to those close to the crown, allowing them to avoid fees and judicial oversight. All of this upset the delicate balance that had allowed the fairs to flourish.

In 1297, France's war with Flanders (the territory of one important group of fair participants) made the trip too dangerous for most merchants. The war also allowed others to take advantage of the Flemish cloth traders without risking repercussion. The series of wars that followed (including the 100 Years War, starting in 1337) only made things worse and helped shift trade routes, making it nearly impossible for the fairs to recover.

There's a lesson there for modern platforms: greed can plant the seeds of your own undoing. There are plenty of modern-day equivalents to the French king's shortsighted exploitation of the fair's merchants. Once you hold a critical position between buyer and seller, market makers suffer from an almost inevitable temptation to profit from it. Uber has been accused of taking a bigger cut of its drivers' fares after convincing them to invest in new cars and luring them to the ride-sharing platform. And Amazon—a notorious driver of hard bargains—eats the lunch of some of its third-party sellers who happen upon a blockbuster product.

That's what researchers Feng Zhu of Harvard and Qihong Liu of the University of Oklahoma found in their analysis of top-selling products on Amazon, where they showed that, in some fraction of these cases, Amazon started stocking the product itself. That was the fate of Jeff Peterson's company, Collectible Supplies, when it struck Amazon gold with its $29.99 Pillow Pets, a line of stuffed toys based on NFL mascots.[18] Through much of 2011, the company was selling one hundred pets a day on Amazon when, with the holiday shopping season on the horizon, daily sales dropped to twenty. A quick search determined the cause. Amazon itself was itself doing a brisk business in Pillow Pets, at prices that undercut those of Collectible Supplies. Peterson tried dropping his prices, but Amazon—both his distributor *and* competitor—was quick to match or beat them.

Zhu and Liu find that when Amazon starts competing with its third-party sellers, they generally try to migrate their sales off Amazon, leaving them less at the mercy of a cold-hearted internet bully. If enough sellers did this, Amazon's lock on internet commerce might start to unravel. Partly for this reason, though, Amazon only picks up about 3 percent of its sellers' top products, according to Zhu and Liu's calculations. Amazon management has presumably decided that doing this strikes a balance between retaining the business of small retailers, who are crucial to the platform's success, and increasing company profits by being more than a pass-through for third parties.[19]

Explore versus Exploit

Sometimes, as platform entrepreneurs will have you believe, they're exploiting business opportunities: technological solutions to heretofore missing markets. That can make life better for all of us. But, as at least some Amazon merchants or Uber drivers might argue, that's not all that platforms are exploiting.

To some extent, both sides are right. Uber is an amazing invention for anyone looking for a ride in a Bay Area suburb on a Saturday night. But give any company enough power over its users, and power tilts toward abuse. If we're to avoid the extremes of just acceding to the visions of platform zealots, or alternatively giving in to their technophobic critics, understanding the logic of what platforms do is surely a good start.

7

MARKETS WITHOUT PRICES

HOW TO FIND A PROM DATE IN
SEVENTEEN EASY STEPS

Take yourself back, if you can, to the eighth-grade dance . . . the awkward cluster of boys stealing uncomfortable glances across a dimly lit gymnasium at the separate but equally awkward cluster of girls. The first slow song of the night—The Police's "Every Breath You Take," in our day—comes lilting over the speakers.

Ah, the middle-school dance. It captures all the pains and anxieties of early adolescence. But strip away the surging hormones, the wispy facial hair, the clumsy dance moves, and what you're left with is a market of sorts: boys and girls looking desperately to match up with one of the scarce resources—that is, a dance partner— available on the other side. (Yes, we recognize the heteronormativity of our scenario but bear with us.)

That may not be how it seems to our market participants on this particular Friday evening in June. In every self-conscious, insecure thirteen-year-old's head rings the eternal question, "Does (s)he like me?" And at that point in life, the threat of rejection— and the accompanying public humiliation—is often enough to make the middle-school slow dance market break down completely.

The search for a partner is further complicated by the fact that, as you're milling about waiting for the middle-school football team captain to ask you for the next dance, Albert, the sweet but dorky boy from science class who has been slowly building up his nerve in the corner, asks you first. Do you make do with Albert, or hold out for the football star, or at least someone better than Albert, knowing that, by waiting, you may end up as the middle-school spinster?

In the past, economists might have ignored this kind of problem, since it fell well outside the scope of the discipline (although nearly all economists experienced the existential angst of some version of this dance, usually in the role of Albert). For much of the economics profession's existence, when economists thought about allocating resources, they focused on two polar options: market prices or a bossy manager or bureaucrat.

Problems like matching middle-school dancers didn't lend itself to the price mechanism, which would have had dancers paying for one another's attention (we're sure you can immediately see the problems with a pay-to-date system). And a Soviet-style central planning committee (made up of who? the popular kids? the principal? concerned parents?) won't go very far in solving the problem either.

The middle-school dance needs a market design makeover, and not one that can be accomplished by market makers of the credit card or Uber variety. Matching resources to wants and needs without prices or money required the development of a different sort of economic model and new thinking on what it means to design a market.

Priceless

Despite the efficiencies the free market might bring, there are lots of things we're not willing to put a price on: a dialysis patient can't buy his way to the top of the transplant wait list, nor do public schools sell off their kindergarten slots to the highest bidders. And God forbid that dating markets should be governed by prices.

When we decide that something is "priceless" (as in we're not going to allow it to be traded based on a price of exchange), the world *does* tend to look a lot like a collection of little Soviet republics. Committees make allocation decisions, and then goods and services are provided on the basis of those decisions. Sometimes, when the committees are wise and well informed, the decisions are good ones. But people in Moscow got an awful lot of stuff they didn't want and not nearly enough of the things they did.

Then again, just as the existence of a price system doesn't guarantee a good outcome—ask investors in Lehman Brothers how price signals in the subprime lending market worked for them—the absence of prices doesn't necessarily guarantee an inefficient one.

There are lots of "market-like" ways of getting people—middle-school students at a dance, daters, school applicants, kidney donors—to express their preferences and to use these wants and desires as inputs into deciding who gets what. Market prices are just one of them—albeit one that's worked really, really well in many cases, since prices capture a desire for one choice over another, and also how strong those preferences are. But how do these preferences get translated into allocations, if not through the wisdom of central planners, or the magic of the market?

The field of market design is, in a sense, the blue-sky-thinking branch of economics. Instead of considering the extent to which prices and markets will or won't be effective in accomplishing a particular task (and how to intervene in traditional markets to make them work better), you start with a task and seek the best way of getting it done.

It gets economists away from thinking inside the box, and a very small one at that. Think about it like this. Suppose you want to help people commute safely and efficiently across the East River, from Brooklyn to Manhattan. Traditional economics is the equivalent of assuming that the only two ways of doing so are bridge or ferry. Mechanism design imagines the broad set of possibilities—zip line, catapult, people mover—then figures out which will work best.

It's what, in technical terms, is called constrained optimization (the same technique Vickrey deployed to determine that the best way to get to work at Columbia was on roller skates). Mechanism designers consider the restrictions imposed by laws, human nature, our sense of right and wrong, and the strategizing that kidney patients, school applicants, and others may engage in to get a better organ or education. And they design a mechanism to best to fulfill society's needs and wants within those constraints.

It's economics as engineering or plumbing rather than economics as physics.

Mechanism Design on Middle-School Dance Night

Matching girls and boys at a school dance may not seem like a particularly pressing social problem to resolve (although dance attendees may beg to differ). But it serves as a stand-in for all sorts of very real and important matchmaking challenges: connecting doctors-in-training to residency programs, aspiring lawyers to clerkships, children to schools, and organs to the right recipients. Each of these situations has its idiosyncrasies. School districts often wish to ensure that siblings can attend the same school; doctors-in-training married to other doctors-in-training may demand to be matched to the same residency program (or at least a residency in the same city); and so forth. And in contrast to a school dance, where each boy gets paired off with exactly one girl, school and residency assignments involve one-to-many matches, where each program takes more than one candidate from the other side of the market.[1]

Although each is complicated in its own way, solutions to these matching problems all build on the same basic mechanism that was presented in a short essay in *American Mathematical Monthly* in 1962. To grasp the basic idea behind the way students in Boston, Paris, and Shanghai are matched to schools, doctors get their residencies, and graduates of the Air Force Academy are assigned to postings, it's easiest to go back to the middle-school gym to figure out a better way of assigning girls and boys to their first dance.[2]

Lloyd Shapley, Matchmaker

In 1962, the mathematician Lloyd Shapley was working at the RAND Corporation (which, you may recall from Chapter 2, along with the Cowles Foundation, helped spur the post–World War II mathematization of economics). Shapley preferred to spend his time thinking about problems like matching girls and boys at the dance rather than the strategic intricacies of the Cold War. We're fortunate that RAND gave him the freedom to do so.

Shapley came from a family of scientists. His father was an eminent astronomer whose claim to fame was showing that the sun (and by extension humanity) existed at the fringes of the Milky Way rather than at its center, as was once thought.

Math came easily to Shapley. He could, in his own telling, compete on an even footing in solving math and logic puzzles with his straight-A brothers who were four and six years older. He went on to become a top math student at Harvard, although his undergraduate career was interrupted during his junior year, in 1943, by the draft. The army shipped him off to central China to serve as a weather forecaster. Shapley's job was to figure out, with at least three days' notice, whether the skies would be clear enough for US planes to fly east to bomb Japan. This turned out to be a tough forecasting problem, as fronts tended to blow down from Siberia, and the Soviets wouldn't let their American allies peek at their weather data. So Shapley cracked the Russians' weather codes, for which he received the Bronze Star, the military's fourth highest individual honor. (Shapley's son remembers hearing his dad say that, far more important than the honor or the accompanying promotion to corporal, were the material comforts that came with a corporal's pay of four dollars a month.[3])

After the end of the war in the Pacific, Shapley returned to Harvard to complete his studies. But he'd gotten sidetracked. Shapley was still a first-rate mathematician and he still loved cracking mathematical puzzles, but he didn't have any clear sense of where these interests should take him. One thing he was fairly sure of was that it wasn't to graduate school in math. At least not yet.

For the field of game theory, the diversion proved fortuitous. Shapley decided to buy some time as he pondered his longer-term aspirations and sent out some résumés along with his transcript of mediocre grades. (In fact, Shapley graduated a year late from Harvard because, despite his perfect grades in math, the university wouldn't award a degree to someone who flunked two courses in his final semester.) One of those résumés went to RAND, which turned out to be a great fit as a place that was willing to indulge a scholar who, according to Shapley, was "not all that disciplined in getting to places on time or going to bed when I should so that I can get up when I should" (which also helps to explain some of those poor grades at Harvard).

RAND had just been launched with an eye to long-range planning of military tactics and weaponry. According to Shapley, the military just decided, "let's not give them an assignment. Give them some money and say, 'You think of some problems and tell us about it.'" This wide-open mandate also allowed his boss to hire—without interview—"crazy students from the math department" like Shapley, and gave RAND's research staff a lot of leeway in how they spent their time.

At some point, the researchers thought it might be interesting to delve into game theory, the branch of mathematics that is used by social scientists to better understand interactions among multiple players, like the Cold War machinations of the Americans and Soviets in the 1950s.

According to Shapley, RAND never tried to "pull me into . . . war-gaming things." He was, as promised, left to do his own thing and proved some important, if esoteric, game theoretic concepts, then went off to Princeton to do more of the same as a PhD student. (His rather esoteric thesis was titled, "Additive and Non-Additive Set Functions.") Although he could surely have gotten a top academic post, Shapley returned to RAND because it had been, and continued to be upon his return, a place where he could focus on his work unencumbered by the distractions of students or classes.

Shapley did keep in touch with some classmates from Princeton, including David Gale, who was teaching at Brown University. Shapley and Gale corresponded regularly by mail, since the phone was too expensive at the time. One day, a letter arrived from Gale containing, essentially, the problem of matching girls and boys at the dance. (In Gale's formulation, the problem involved producing roommate pairings from two groups.) In his letter, Gale wondered whether it was possible to produce a set of matches that were "stable" in the sense that, given their assigned matches, there isn't a boy and girl who would want to sneak off because they'd be happier with one another than the partner they received via the match. Gale didn't think so. Shapley wasn't so sure. He recalled opening the letter around noon. He thought about it for a while, wrote out what he thought was a solution, and by the end of the afternoon an answer was in an envelope and on its way to Gale's office in Providence.

Deferred Acceptance at the Middle School Dance

Together, the two mathematicians refined and wrote up Shapley's response in a paper titled "College Admissions and the Stability of Marriage." It initially suffered the fate of so many truly original ideas: it was rejected by the establishment. Reviewers found it too simple. And in a sense they were right. As Gale and Shapley explain at the outset, their argument is "carried out not in mathematical symbols but in ordinary English; there are no obscure or technical terms. Knowledge of calculus is not presupposed. In fact, one hardly needs to know how to count."

Their explanation goes something like this (and when we say "something like this" we really mean it; Gale and Shapley's paper is scarcely more complicated than what we've written below). Let's return to the middle-school gym and assume that, given social conventions, boys do the asking and girls simply respond with a yes or a no. Before getting started, we'll give each girl a chance to list, in her own mind, every middle-school boy in order of preference, starting with the middle-school dreamboat on down. Each boy similarly ranks all the girls.

Now, let's start matching. Each boy crosses the floor to stand in front of the girl of his dreams, his first choice. Some girls will have a long row of suitors to pick among; others won't have any at all. Any girl with at least one boy to choose from gets to pick her favorite, and he gets to stand beside her—at least for now. He's her backup guy.

At this point, there are plenty of boys that have been spurned by their first choice; each will look to the second name on his list and queue up in front of her. Lots will end up in front of a girl that already has a partner—her backup guy, remember. If, among a girl's new arrivals, there's someone better than her fallback option, she'll swap him in and return the old backup to the "market."

Then we just let the process repeat itself. Any boys that aren't currently paired off work their way down their lists, and any girls that have had at least one suitor keep a partner "in reserve," while waiting to see if a boy that ranks higher on her list appears in her queue. This goes on until all boys and girls find matches (or until boys have run far enough down their lists that they'd rather just sulk on the sidelines than find themselves a partner).

Gale and Shapley called it the "deferred acceptance" algorithm— deferred in the sense that each girl gets to keep a backup date but defers her acceptance of him until she's had a chance to see what other prospects might appear.

What makes deferred acceptance so useful as a clearinghouse for dates and many other matching problems is its stability: once it's run its course, there won't be a boy-girl pair eying one another from across the room, wishing they could be together. How did Shapley know this to be true? By definition, a boy would only want to trade his final match for someone who was higher on his list. Under deferred acceptance, he's already tried his luck with every higher-ranked girl, and they've all rejected him. And why did they reject him? Because they already had a better backup option when he arrived (and could only have "traded up" since then). So among the girls for whom he'd forgo his final match, there won't be any takers.

Making up problems and trying to solve them is just what mathematicians do. They aren't necessarily interested in building better mousetraps or figuring out a strategic response to the Soviet nuclear threat. In this case, though, Gale and Shapley's solution has turned out to be of immense practical value because some very important allocation problems look very similar to matching dancers in the gym.

Take the problem of matching students to schools in New York (or Paris or Shanghai or any one of the many other cities that use a variant on deferred acceptance to make school assignments). To fill their kindergarten slots, each principal submits to the superintendent an ordered list of her choice of students. (In practice, the principal's preferences are usually dictated by considerations mandated by the school board, with priorities for siblings and students living nearby. As far as the algorithm is concerned, it makes no difference where the preference ordering comes from.)

Each student (or his parents) sends in a ranking of schools. The only difference between the school-dance match and the kindergarten match is that, in each round, schools fill as many of their available seats as they can with the students lining up to get in and send the rest back to the market to work down their lists (as compared to the dance, where matching is one boy for one girl).

And while visualizing students migrating around the school gym in search of a dance partner may be useful in grasping the mechanics behind Gale and Shapley's algorithm, in practice there's no need for it. Once each market participant has submitted his or her list, the deferred acceptance algorithm takes care of the rest. Why magnify the awkwardness of adolescence through a real-life multiround popularity contest? If students go online to submit their rankings the morning of the dance, they'll get an assigned match by lunchtime. Similarly, once the superintendent has rankings from schools and students, a computer program crunches the numbers and sends back a set of class assignments.

Not everyone gets exactly what he or she wants. But life rarely sees a John Hughes movie ending, where Sam ends up with Jake, and Ted gets to drive Caroline home in the Rolls Royce. There's only one prom queen, and for better or worse, odds are she's dancing with the captain of the football team. But that's also the wrong standard by which to judge the success of Gale and Shapley's match. Economics is all about allocating *scarce* goods under conditions of infinite desires. As harsh as it sounds, the pimple-faced kid with limited prospects is doing the best he can with what Gale and Shapley offer him.

What deferred acceptance *can* ensure is that once the matches are set, no one wants to go outside the system in search of a better match—that was what Shapley proved one afternoon in 1961. Without stability, the whole system can easily unravel as more and more dancers are abandoned by their partners for better prospects.

This may have you asking what's wrong with the old-fashioned approach of just having boys and girls ask each other to the dance, which is essentially what goes on when couples start opting out of the match. This is what's called a decentralized match. And decentralized matches, it turns out, have an unhappy history of unraveling in lots of situations.

To understand why, let's go back to the middle-school gym. If there's no dating clearinghouse to pair off couples at the dance itself, a boy needs to start planning ahead: he who hesitates till the day of the dance will be dateless. So a bunch of reasonably forward-looking adolescents are going to do their asking the day before. But why take the chance that you'll already have been pre-empted? Better get to the girl you really want to ask *two* days before the dance. You see where this is going—in a decentralized match where both sides are worried about being desperate and dateless by the time the main event arrives, the "market" unravels backward, with earlier and earlier attempts at locking in a match. Given the capriciousness of middle-school romance, you might get locked into a date with the football captain before you come to your senses and realize that Albert is your true crush. In the same way, first-year law students likely have no idea what they want to do with their lives, so locking them into a postgraduation job early on can lead to costly, hard-to-reverse career decisions.

It was exactly this kind of unraveling that was the undoing of the market for clerkships with federal judges, where it wasn't unheard of for better students to get "exploding" (that is, time-sensitive) offers in their first year of law school. Before judges began making offers earlier and earlier to preempt one another, it was possible for students to wait until partway through the third (and final) law school year before receiving and responding to clerkship offers. And it left potential clerks early in their law school careers needing to commit to an offer before exploring other options—or even knowing what kind of law they wished to practice.

It happened to the market for slots at sororities, too, which used to be reserved for college seniors, until popular girls started getting invitations to join at the start of their junior, then sophomore, then freshman year. (According to market design guru Al Roth, one theory holds that the term "fraternity/sorority rush," which today describes the process by which sororities and fraternities recruit new members, comes from the frenzied competition among sororities to lock in new members.[4]) It's what prompted medical residency programs to develop a centralized clearinghouse in the 1940s to fend off students receiving exploding offers before they were done with their intro to anatomy course.

These allocation problems all now have centralized clearing-houses, many designed with the basic deferred acceptance algo-rithm as their foundations. But that's really all that Gale and

Shapley provided: a conceptual framework that market designers have, for several decades now, been applying, evaluating, and refining. They've learned from its successes and, unfortunately, learned even more from its inevitable failures: modeling real-life exchanges is an imprecise, iterative process in which many of us find ourselves as experimental subjects.

The Complicated Job of Engineering Matches

Market designer Al Roth likes to use a bridge-building metaphor to explain the contrast between his own work and that of design pioneers like Shapley. Suppose you want to build a suspension bridge connecting Brooklyn and Manhattan. In confronting decisions like where to place the suspension cables and how thick each should be, you'd better have paid attention in physics class. Things like Euler's buckling equation, which provides the maximum axial load that a long, slender, ideal column can carry before it crumples, are important background knowledge for bridge builders to be. But the theoretical constructs involving "ideal" columns will take you only so far. A bridge that stands in theory may, in practice, sink into the riverbed or ripple with wave-like undulations when the wind blows just so. (If you want to see a dramatic example, go to YouTube and watch the Tacoma Narrows Bridge collapse.)

Every bridge presents its own unique design challenges—the soil, the way the river flows, the weather, the wear and tear of cars and trucks speeding to and fro. You start with Isaac Newton and Leonhard Euler, but had better take into account the complexities of each situation even if it doesn't allow you to derive a simple "final answer."

That makes bridge engineering a messier process, involving extended computer simulations, site visits to scope out the riverbank, analysis of soil samples, and stress testing scale models in a wind tunnel. All of this testing and modeling might help you predict whether cars will start flying off the roadway when a storm blows in.

A parallel set of challenges confronts market engineers. The elegant argument that Gale and Shapley spelled out for matching dancers at a dance can easily be extended to circumstances where students apply to schools looking to fill kindergarten slots (where each school gets to hold a backup student for each available slot, rather than the single backup guy that each girl at the dance keeps in reserve). But school boards rarely allow parental preferences alone to determine school assignments. Budget constraints might impose limits on how many students get bused to school, which in turn dictates that priority be given to applicants from a school's "walk zone"; siblings need to be matched as a group so there's no need for parents to shuttle from school to school; concerns over diversity may require that some slots in rich neighborhoods be filled with lower-income students.

When you throw in these many constraints, there isn't going to be any easy formula—an economics equivalent of Euler's buckling equation—that you can use for school assignments (even assuming that parents have a clear understanding of the rules governing the match process, and or even know their own preferences). Market designers, like their civil engineering counterparts, run experiments, tinker with rules, simulate the effects, and eventually hope that it leads to a final product that does a reasonable job of satisfying the wants and desires of both parents and the school board. And as with each new bridge that's constructed, we hope to learn a little more about how to design the next one a little better.

That also leaves an unnerving aspect to this process of learning by designing. No matter how hard you try to iron out any contingencies in wind tunnels or computer models, you never quite know what will happen when the design gets stress-tested by real-world conditions. Every once in a while, a bridge designed to withstand hurricanes finds it isn't hurricane-proof after all, and the best-laid school assignment mechanism, it turns out, leaves dissatisfied students and principals in its wake. Like it or not, drivers on the newly constructed Bay Bridge in San Francisco are, in a very small way, participating in a bridge designer's experiment, much as kindergartners in Boston are guinea pigs in the process of designing better ways of assigning students to schools.

Two Kinds of Sick Schools

As former New York Department of Education administrator Neil Dorosin puts it, there are essentially two ways that organizations can be sick. The first involves mild symptoms that give you a sense that something might be wrong. You have trouble sleeping, the occasional headache; it could be high blood pressure. But there's no need to run to the emergency room. And then there's debilitating chest pain.[5]

When Dorosin took a job at the New York Department of Education in the mid-2000s, it was having the organizational equivalent of a heart attack. The cause of the coronary was a malfunctioning school assignment system for local fourteen-year-olds. The multi-round process was, at its best, convoluted, confusing, and drawn out. In theory, it looks clean and simple. In each round, schools sent out acceptances and wait-list positions to students, who then responded yea or nay. Things then proceeded to the next round, with yet more offers from schools with any remaining scats to students still unassigned or wait-listed, followed again by student responses, and so on.

According to Dorosin, this benign description obscures the actual state of dysfunction, as it ignores the intense strategizing and lobbying that was going on behind the scenes. Each principal got to see how students had ranked his school before making any offers, and it was common for desirable schools to only accept applicants that ranked them as their top choice. And among applicants that ranked a school first, the ones who actually got in were those who had the knowledge and wherewithal to lobby the principal for one of the scarce slots.

Some kids—the smart ones who knew how to navigate this high school admissions free-for-all—got multiple offers. At the same time, over a third of the city's eighth graders didn't get matched at all and were simply handed a school assignment that had nothing to do with their preferences or abilities.

Dorosin saw this problem firsthand as an eighth-grade science teacher in the South Bronx in the mid-1990s. Every year a range of students came into his classroom. Some were good at physics; others struggled. Some showed up to class and paid attention; others, not so much. Yet when high school assignments were handed out in his homeroom at the end of the year, all his students got funneled into the same low-performing neighborhood schools. When he went to work for the Department of Education's central administration, hired by the reform-minded schools chancellor Joel Klein, he found himself part of a group tasked with resuscitating New York's ailing school assignment process.

At around the same time Dorosin and his colleagues were consulting with market design experts on fixing the situation in New York, school officials in Boston had started to look at market design as a solution to their own school-match woes—although the Boston school system only had a slight headache compared to NYC's cardiac arrest. A mechanism design expert at Boston College, Tayfun Sönmez, had been hounding the city's school board for years with proposals on how to improve student assignments using a match based on deferred acceptance. His overtures had been consistently ignored. That changed in 2003 when the *Boston Globe* ran a story, "School assignment flaws detailed: Two economists study problem, offer relief," based on some of Sönmez's research. Public school leaders finally started paying attention.[6]

Because the problems in Boston were more of the headache and dizziness variety, it had been easy enough to ignore advice on how to get better. Still, the system had a basic, well-recognized flaw that Gale and Shapley's algorithm had been shown to solve: the assignment process forced students, or rather their parents, to strategize on how to rank schools. In a nutshell, the Boston mechanism had focused on assigning as many students as possible to their first-choice school. So it used an algorithm that started by placing all students at their top choice, subject to priorities imposed by the school board. These priorities aimed to minimize the need for busing by placing kids in their walk zone schools and also to promote racial and socioeconomic diversity.

For popular schools with an excess of first-choice applicants, the scarce slots would be assigned by lottery, with the applicants who drew low numbers put back in the pool to be placed elsewhere. Now here's the problem: imagine you know your first choice is going to be hugely oversubscribed, while the next-best option, which you like almost as much, is unlikely to get a flood of applicants. Why take the chance that your second-choice school will get filled up at the end of the first round? Better just to put your second choice at the top of your list and go with the safer bet. But once you start thinking like this, there are further layers of calculation. How many *other* parents will go through the same line of reasoning, making your second choice a less-than-safe option? And what if it turns out that your first choice isn't oversubscribed after all? You get the school match equivalent of buyer's regret.

This led to a slow, grinding discontent and apprehension and a sense of an unequal playing field in the admissions game, albeit on a lesser scale than in New York. Well-informed and involved parents knew to game the system and discussed among themselves how best to do so. At a 2003 parents' group meeting in Boston's West Zone, the minutes included the following advice: "[F]ind a school you like that is undersubscribed and put it as a top choice, OR, find a school that you like that is popular and put it as a first choice and find a school that is less popular for a 'safe' second choice."[7]

A mechanism that doesn't require this sort of anxiety-filled overthinking is called "strategy-proof" and it had been shown decades earlier that Gale and Shapley's deferred acceptance method satisfied this property. You can't do any better than list your true school preferences and let the algorithm do the rest.

To make a long story shorter (there is, after all, no such thing as a short story in the annals of school reform), after years of meetings, lobbying by all sides, presentation of proposals and counterproposals, and yet more lobbying and politicking, Boston schools adopted a version of deferred acceptance in 2006. (The New York school system, which was much more desperately in need of change, had already adopted a deferred acceptance–based system three years earlier.) Students listed up to six schools, in order of preference. The rankings that each school assigned to students were dictated by school board priorities: preference was given to applicants with siblings, and half of all seats were reserved for walk zone students who lived within a mile of the school.

Now, the reasoning went, applicants no longer had to confer at parent association meetings on how best to game the assignment process. Parents who didn't have the time, inclination, or access to well-informed parent association gossip wouldn't be disadvantaged. By all accounts, at least by this measure the new school match was a success. But it turned out that the new system just traded one set of problems for another.

In 2011, the *Boston Globe* documented the travails of individual families that were on the receiving end of Boston's version of Gale and Shapley's algorithm. The *Globe* series, collectively titled "Inside the School Assignment Maze," followed parents and kids through each step in the assignment process. One, titled "Selection process starts with choices, ends with luck," conveyed the sense among parents that the system had the mere illusion of choice and all too often led to capricious and uneven results ("Relief, dismay, even guilt greet student placements"). While 50 percent of all seats were reserved for walk zone families, the school board had anticipated that many more than half of the students at any school would come from nearby. But somehow, whatever was going on inside the algorithmic black box that made assignments, things didn't seem to be working out that way ("In school lottery, living close simply isn't enough"), leading to splintered communities ("A daily diaspora, a scattered street") and much higher than expected busing costs ("The high price of school assignment").[8]

The fact that not all parents got exactly what they wanted for their children isn't necessarily a sign of a broken assignment mechanism. No mechanism could deliver that outcome, after all. Just as not everyone gets to dance with the prom queen, there are only so many students that you can fit in the kindergarten class at the very best schools. At the risk of repeating ourselves, the very definition of economics is figuring out how to do the best you can with the resources you've got. A better assignment mechanism isn't going to improve the quality of Boston's schools, which, by all accounts, weren't that great. It merely reshuffles students among them in a way that should leave parents happier on average than before. As long as there are less-than-stellar resources to be parceled out among those with unlimited wants, there will be griping and complaining.

Yet by the time the *Globe* stories came out, it was clear that this wasn't merely a case of unreasonable parental expectations. Some of the very same economists that designed the match in the first place posted a study that proved mathematically why the algorithm failed to assign more students to nearby schools. Indeed, their simulations indicated that just as many students would have been assigned to nearby schools if there had been no walk zone priority at all. Why did this happen?

The explanation is subtle, so bear with us for just a moment. But its subtlety can also help you appreciate why market designers may have missed it on first pass. In putting Gale and Shapley's algorithm into practice, students ranked each school. The market designers thought of district priorities as being like schools' rankings of students. So just as each girl in the middle-school gym would have her suitors line up in order, a school would accept each child in order of priority based on school zone, income, and so forth. Of course, it was possible that more students would apply from a priority group than the school had slots for. More than 50 percent of neighborhood kids would often put their walk zone school first. To break ties, the assignment algorithm gave each student a lottery number at the very beginning of the process, with higher numbers getting to line up near the front of the queue of applicants that otherwise had the same priority.

This turned out to be the system's undoing. To understand why, think of a student who gets a high lottery number and ranks his walk zone school first. He, along with all the other local kids who got lucky numbers, will be at the front of the walk zone queue and will fill up the 50 percent walk zone quota. Which walk zone students will be left at this point? Just the ones that were assigned low lottery numbers. They're then thrown in with everyone outside the walk zone who ranked the school first. Since this second group has yet to be winnowed of all its high lottery students, the walk zone kids are mostly going to be outranked by outside applicants. It may seem counterintuitive at first, but a simple change would have eliminated this problem. If schools had first filled up their "open" slots with the highest-ranked applicants, a lot more walk zone students would have gotten in. Why? Because those high lottery walk zone kids will now be filling up the open slots, leaving the walk zone priority seats for other nearby students who didn't draw high numbers in the school assignment lottery.

So that's it: a subtle and, indeed, counterintuitive difference in how seats are filled essentially undid one of the main objectives of the Boston school assignment. But it also highlights how the specifics of the problem the designers are trying solve really matter; there is no one-size-fits-all solution.

By 2012, Boston parents had had enough. In response, the school board floated a number of internally generated ideas for reforming the school assignment process—again. These were not well received; a Harvard study argued that all of the proposals would only exacerbate the current system's problems. In what some say was an act of desperation, they gave an open call for presentations on how to fix the school assignment mess.

The public-at-large submitted about a dozen proposals. Some were from political candidates aiming to promote their platforms, and a handful were from community activists. Finally, a twenty-four-year-old PhD student in operations at MIT, Peng Shi, signed up to present his solution. Shi had been a devoted attendee of the public meetings to discuss school assignment reform, chatting with parents and activists to better understand the sources of dissatisfaction with the current system and what sorts of changes would be palatable to them.

Shi's initial proposal involved an attempt to, in his words, "define equality of access rigorously." Based on his rigorous definition, he devised a solution that involved linear programming methods (a branch of mathematical optimization) to minimize the distance traveled by Boston students subject to an equitable access constraint. If this is incomprehensible to you, the committee shared your reaction. One school committee member pulled Shi aside later and explained that, if you want something to actually get implemented, you had better be able to explain it to a fifth grader.

But the committee *did* like Shi's approach of seriously modeling the two things that Boston parents cared about—distance and access—and asked him to make another pitch. He came back with a plan that limited parents' options to nearby schools, plus a small number of other "high quality" schools that were closest to the student's home. This balanced the needs of access to good schools for all (a student far from any decent options would get a wider radius to choose within) with the imperative of assigning kids close to home. And it was a simple enough approach that parents, and probably their kindergartners as well, could understand how it worked and the choices available to them.

Did Shi throw the deferred acceptance baby out with the old school assignment bathwater? Not at all. Deferred acceptance is still the algorithm that governs the assignment of students to schools once they've submitted their rankings of each of the options available to them. But he's managed to insert it into a more transparent and effective mechanism.

This is how science—and society—progresses. We make well-meaning attempts at socially improving innovations. Sometimes they work exactly as we had hoped: the deferred acceptance high school match in New York is still running today in essentially its original form. More often there are tweaks and adjustments along the way, or as was the case in Boston, we're blindsided by something serious enough that we need to return to the drawing board. But hopefully we return to it a good deal wiser than before.

For Boston parents, it is surely hard to be so Zen about this process of experimentation and reinvention. It's never a great feeling to be on the receiving end of someone else's tinkering.

And that is the situation on a larger scale that most of us find ourselves in: subject to tinkering from all quarters. But unlike both the New York and Boston school system experiments, it's not clear, beyond some internet company's profits, what's being optimized. And if the experiment fails? Well, the experimenters tend to be true believers anyway and won't be deterred by the little mess they leave behind. For most market innovations, we won't have a school board or any other higher authority to go to with our grievances.

8

LETTING MARKETS WORK

HOW A HARDCORE SOCIALIST LEARNED TO STOP WORRYING AND LOVE THE MARKET

A funny thing happened when economist Jonas Vlachos's kids went back to their government-run school in Sweden after summer vacation in 2012. Vlachos's family lived a fifteen-minute walk from his son's elementary school, so to get there for the nine o'clock bell, his son left the first morning at a little before eight forty-five. The next day he left a little earlier, and even earlier the day after that. Within a week or two, Vlachos Junior was leaving an hour before the opening bell.

What, Vlachos Senior wondered, was going on? It turned out that there weren't quite enough coat hooks at the back of his classroom to go around, and later arrivals had to leave their jackets crumpled on a bench (apparently a source of grade school ignominy for order-loving Swedes). So the "market" for coat hooks began to unravel backward in much the same way that, in the absence of a centralized clearinghouse, residency programs and judges raced to recruit medical and law students earlier and earlier.

Now, Jonas Vlachos is hardly an apologist for the glories of free enterprise and markets. He's from Sweden, for one thing, and Scandinavians are known worldwide for their love of big taxes and big government. More personally, Vlachos has been a vocal critic of his country's market-like approach to education, which is based in part on the school choice vision laid out by Milton Friedman, an icon of laissez-faire ideology. Vlachos's own kids go to good old-fashioned government-run schools rather than the privately owned voucher ones that exist alongside them.

Vlachos had argued that markets were, in many ways, ill suited to serving the educational needs of Swedish students. The private voucher schools he observed in Stockholm were excessively motivated to cut costs to boost profits, to manipulate test scores to attract more students and gain greater prestige, and to skim off the best students by locating or recruiting in prosperous neighborhoods.

But assigning coat hooks? That was a simple job that the market could solve. Vlachos, fed up with his son's growing coat-hook anxieties and ever-earlier departures, made this argument one evening to his wife: Why not auction off hook spots to the highest bidders? Parents that didn't want to deal with getting their kids out the door an hour earlier would bid the most. Kids who were at peace with the idea of their jackets crumpled on a bench wouldn't bid at all. All the children came from reasonably well-off homes so most parents could afford to put in a bid, and even if it weren't so, the bids of lower-income parents could be subsidized.

Then, the "coat-tax" proceeds could be used to finance a field trip or to purchase something for the classroom beyond the government-issue materials. It was win-win.

Vlachos's wife quite sensibly told his husband to keep his coat-hook auction ideas to himself, anticipating that his well-meaning (if only half-serious) suggestion wouldn't be well received by his fellow parents. Auctioning off classroom coat hooks isn't just offensive to Swedish sensibilities: on hearing this story most people (or at least noneconomists) think Vlachos sounds socially inept, obnoxious, stupid, or all of the above (which he isn't, for the record). In a way, though, it's hard to see why: he merely suggested that we use a fair and efficient market mechanism to solve a coat-hook allocation problem.

But there are some problems that most people would leave as problems rather than have the market provide a solution.

The free market has long had an image problem, and a well-deserved one at that. Markets aren't well suited to some things—voucher schools in Sweden, some would argue. But they are good for others, like assigning school hooks. Unfortunately, it's easy to mistake circumstances that look like coat hooks for circumstances that look like misguided voucher programs, especially if you hold a dim view of markets to begin with.

Why does this concern us? Because that image problem gets in the way of using markets to do some good for society. Markets are a means of resource allocation, and often a really effective one at that. But they're not good for everything—or at least not without a lot of engineering and tweaking. That's something both free-market advocates, as well as those who find markets wholly repugnant, need to hear.

We need to develop the wisdom to know when to deploy the market in some situations and not in others. This requires developing a better understanding of what markets can and can't accomplish and entertaining their strengths and shortcomings with an open mind. What we'd like to leave you with is, in a way, a very old and at this point familiar idea: the need to appreciate the benefits of market efficiency and trade them off against the potential for market failure.

But there are also situations where we might reasonably decide that, while markets might create more GDP and even distribute it more equally, we'd still rather find some other way of doing things. It might be because we don't care to put a price on everything, or it may be because we don't like what the market will do to us as individuals and a society.

In Princeton sociologist Viviana Zelizer's classic *Morals and Markets: The Development of Life Insurance in the United States*, she traces the rise of the life insurance business in the 1840s. In the earlier part of the nineteenth century, life insurance was condemned as a "strictly financial evaluation of human life" that blurred the boundary between spiritual and commercial matters. Enterprising insurance salesmen went about altering these attitudes toward death and dying, advocating, for example, for the idea of a "good death" that would show concern for loved ones beyond the grave. These merchants of a good death also made fortunes for themselves in the process.[1]

Maybe this was a good thing for society. But we need to make these decisions for ourselves: instead of being subject to the whims of economists and businesses (where we currently find ourselves), if we have a better sense of where markets work, and why, and how, and in what form, then we can decide when we want to use them rather than be used by them.

Mr. Socialist, Meet the Market

Canice Prendergast is an economics professor at the University of Chicago's Booth School of Business. He works in the language of dense mathematical models that aim to clarify why, for example, service at airport security is so dismal and why—you may not be pleased to hear—that might actually be a good thing. (Because a few of the Department of Homeland Security's "customers" may be bomb-carrying terrorists, so it's not exactly a customer-is-always-right setting.) He's a serious enough art collector that when Booth built itself a $125 million campus across the way from Frank Lloyd Wright's landmark Robie House, Prendergast was put in charge of a million-dollar budget for decorating its courtyards and hallways. Instead of the usual array of bland landscapes and oil paintings of old white men in suits that populate the walls of many a business school or corporate office, Booth's walls are filled with abstract, conceptual works that challenge and often mystify its faculty and students. (Many, it seems, aren't even aware it's art. According to a local paper, "One of the major threats to the pieces is the back-packs and coffee cups of negligent students who don't realize they are working around priceless works of art."[2])

Some years ago, Prendergast's colleague, Robert Hamada, invited him to join a working group at America's Second Harvest (now called Feeding America), a clearinghouse that takes surplus food from grocery stores, food producers, and farms and distributes it among a network of food banks across the country. The two economists were to be joined by two other Chicago Booth professors, operations professor Don Eisenstein and an expert in organizational behavior, Harry Davis.

As with many successful organizations, Second Harvest has its founding legend, in this case the story of John van Hengel, a retired businessman working at a Phoenix soup kitchen. As the organization states on its homepage, "One day, [van Hengel] met a desperate mother who regularly rummaged through grocery store garbage bins to find food for her children. She suggested that there should be a place where, instead of being thrown out, discarded food could be stored for people to pick up—similar to the way 'banks' store money for future use. With that, an industry was born." After inventing the food bank industry, van Hengel went on to found Second Harvest to better allocate donations across the various food banks that were popping up around the country.

By the time Prendergast and his colleagues appeared on the scene, the clearinghouse worked something like this: A donor company, say Kraft, would notify Second Harvest that a load of Macaroni & Cheese was available for pickup. Second Harvest management would then offer the shipment to one of the two hundred affiliates around the country based on need, proximity to the pickup locale, and a formula that dictated how many pounds of donations each food bank was entitled to each year. The local food banks were responsible for shipping the donation. Once the food arrived at the affiliate's warehouse, volunteers sorted it, entered it into a computerized grocery list, and made it available for local charities that served the hungry and poor.

By all accounts, it was a reasonably well-designed and well-functioning system. By 2004, Second Harvest was shipping a truly remarkable 1.8 billion pounds of food. GuideStar, a charity watchdog group, gave Second Harvard a rating of four stars out of a possible four.

It may have been a reasonably good setup, but far from optimized. Food banks might provide feedback on their likes and dislikes, but at its core, the Second Harvest allocation still resembled 1960s-era Chinese central planning (which, free-market economists will note, helped to cause the Great Famine of 1959–1961). Early on, Prendergast and his colleagues brought up the idea of using something like a market instead.

As Prendergast imagined it, the Second Harvest market currency would be made-up points, or shares, that would be distributed among the couple of hundred member food banks. These made-up shares could then be bid on food donations as they arrived in Second Harvest's system each day. In a sense, nothing would change.

Kraft would offer a container load of Mac & Cheese, and it would be allocated to a food bank affiliate to feed the hungry. But instead of being distributed by Second Harvest's central office, the food bank that wanted it the most would express that preference by parting with precious shares to get it.

The nine food bank presidents who comprised the rest of the working group did not all greet the idea of using markets to fix their not-really-broken system with a standing ovation. It may not have helped that the pitch came from a group of University of Chicago economists, whose ranks include libertarian extremists like Milton Friedman (of school-voucher fame) and Gene "Efficient Markets" Fama. Prendergast recalls that at some point during the preliminary discussions, John Arnold, then president of the West Michigan Food Bank, stood up and announced, "Look, I've got to tell you guys. I'm a card-carrying member of the American Socialist Party. I was a conscientious objector. I have no interest in using your f***ing market."

From where the socialist, peace-loving Arnold sat, markets looked, first and foremost, like institutions of exploitation, not allocation. That's why he worked for a food bank rather than Monsanto or the Chicago Mercantile Exchange. But as far as Prendergast and his colleagues were concerned, Arnold's attitude was misguided. Under their proposed system, no money was to change hands. Kraft, Krogers, and others were donating their food, not selling it (though they did receive a tax write-off), and America's Second Harvest, itself a charity, wasn't taking any cut of the proceeds.

But it didn't look so benign from Arnold's office in Comstock Park, where it seemed more like the market was what created the problems of hunger and homelessness he was fighting against. The market somehow allowed executives in Detroit to earn seven figure salaries they didn't deserve to buy million-dollar homes they didn't need, while he struggled to keep from getting buried under the millions of pounds of groceries that he distributed each year with barely enough funding to hire a single full-time administrator to help him out. (Arnold and his assistant together earned barely more than $100,000 a year between the two of them—enough for a comfortable life in the Midwest, but practically a rounding error for a corporation's executive payroll.) If life wasn't fair, the market was at least partly to blame. Just as some Swedes saw the market as wrong for schools and concluded it wasn't useful for coat hooks, Arnold saw the way markets served as a vehicle of exploitation and lost sight of their potential usefulness in food distribution.

The main barrier to improving Second Harvest's distribution system, it seemed, wasn't devising an efficient market. The bigger challenge was making it seem fair to Arnold's socialist sensibilities. The only way the invisible hand was going to work its magic for Second Harvest was if Arnold could see, as a bit player in the national market for food aid, what was in it for him and for everyone else too.

Prendergast is modest about his accomplishments. When we told some of his economics colleagues about his work with Second Harvest, none of them had heard about it. And he is notably understated in describing his contribution to making Second Harvest's food donation market the success that it became; he gives most of the credit to Harry Davis.

Among social scientists, economists have a reputation of being "undersocialized." It's not just that we're awkward and ill mannered (although that's true at times as well). The deeper critique is that economic models fail to capture the nuances of human relations. Davis was trained in sociology (what many economists would call an "oversocialized" field). Davis thought a lot about human relationships: he was a good listener, he was able to draw out the concerns that Arnold had, and he was able to work with his market-minded colleagues to devise a system that addressed them.

Arnold's fear wasn't that Kraft or General Mills would somehow abuse a Second Harvest market. Instead, he was worried about exploitation by other food banks. He and his assistant did everything at the West Michigan Food Bank, from helping volunteers stock shelves to filing their own tax returns. (If you look them up on GuideStar, you'll see they're filled in by hand.) They didn't have time to track bids in an eBay-style auction for food donations, and they didn't have the money to hire someone to do it for them. Second Harvest affiliates in Chicago, New York, and LA—titans of the food bank world—had dozens of staff members and hundreds of volunteers to draw on to monitor auctions in real time, possibly swooping in at the last moment to snatch the choicest shipments.

And that's presuming Arnold ever had a shot at a truckload of Skippy at all. Under the initial proposal, shares were to be allocated based on the poverty headcount in each affiliate's service area. The same food banks with the staff to track food auctions in real time were also located in population-dense urban centers, which would entitle them to a disproportionate allocation of shares. They'd always end up getting the good stuff. Arnold was actually worried that he might never get any food at all, given that the "rich" big-city food banks would always have a full enough war chest to outbid him.

Finally, even if Arnold did have the time and shares to compete with the big boys, how would he know what to bid? New York was distributing container-loads of peanut butter and jelly every month. Arnold could last half a year with one shipment. So when it came time to getting more, how would he know how high to bid? Not only would he have fewer points than larger food banks, he also would probably end up wasting them by overbidding.

The design of Second Harvest's market took these and other anxieties over potential inequities between large and small food banks into account. Instead of an eBay-style system of shipments that appeared and expired in real time based on the flow of donations, offers accumulated throughout the day. Then, the following morning, each food bank would receive the full list of items for bid to consider. Every food bank would have the opportunity to review the listings and make its best offer on each one through a sealed-bid auction. The winning bidder would send a truck to collect the donation, and the shares from its winning bid would get split up among all two hundred food banks in the Second Harvest network.

This last point might not seem like a big deal: if everyone gets some extra shares, then it won't make anyone richer; it'll simply make prices rise through more aggressive bidding. But, Prendergast recalled, it totally changed the psychology of losing an auction from "the rich bastard outbid me again" to "that chump overpaid again!"

They settled on an initial money supply of ten million shares and allowed bidders to squirrel away their currency to make a single big purchase, which was of particular value to the smaller food banks.

One unexpected consequence of becoming a market designer was that Prendergast found himself playing the role of central banker. Central bankers manage money supply, and they do so in large part to keep prices steady. Price stability was also a major concern of small food banks: since they made relatively infrequent purchases, historical prices provided them with guidance on how much to bid.

For the Federal Reserve (the United States's central bank), this involves too many complications to enumerate here—from figuring out how many one hundred dollar bills in circulation are hiding under Russian mobsters' floorboards to estimating the rate at which bills flow through the economy to assessing investors' beliefs about future money supply (which may make them spend, or stuff more bills in mattresses), and so on and so forth.

Prendergast faced many similar challenges in managing Second Harvest's economy, albeit on a much smaller scale. Food bank presidents, it turned out, were hoarders of shares. To keep the market from dipping into a deflationary spiral, in the early days in particular, Prendergast needed to pump extra shares into the market. There was also the ebb and flow of goods into the market to consider. Some days, Kraft might dump half a dozen container-loads of Mac & Cheese into circulation; other days there'd be none. If everyone used their points to bid on Mac & Cheese, the prices of, say, potato chips and broccoli, would plummet. So extra shares would need to be put into circulation to prop up prices—lest Arnold see last week's lower price of potato chips and bid too timidly on them. Similarly, in a dry spell of donations, shares would be withdrawn from the market.

Another unanticipated consequence of "marketizing" food distribution—this one positive—is that prices gave Second Harvest's leadership a sense of what kinds of donations were most valued by affiliates. In a free-market economy, these market signals would motivate suppliers to ramp up production of whatever might be popular or motivate new entrants to enter the popular market.

For Second Harvest, prices revealed that peanut butter and noodles were the two food types most valued by food charities. Frozen chicken wasn't far behind. They're all storable, calorie-dense, reasonably nutritious foods that people will actually eat. What was popular among food banks might not have mattered to the producers, but it motivated the central office at Second Harvest to hunt more aggressively for donors of frozen chicken and peanut butter, less so for potatoes, and least of all for potato chips. In fact, chips, a bulky, fragile junk food, are so little valued by food banks that sometimes their prices turn negative, so a food bank receives shares in exchange for the cost and hassle of picking up the shipment. Kale and broccoli were better than Doritos, but not by much; you don't end up feeding the hungry if all you give them is stuff they can't cook or won't eat.

(We asked Prendergast why Second Harvest even accepts potato chip donations, or why they don't just send a garbage truck instead of a delivery van and pulverize them on site. He pointed out the need to maintain their relationships with the very same chip-producing donors who also make the peanut butter, chicken, and pasta that food banks want and need. If Second Harvest needed to absorb a shipment of chips to keep big agriculture happy, so be it.)

What did John Arnold of the West Michigan Food Bank think of the shift to a food distribution market? He quickly went from being its chief skeptic to one of its most enthusiastic users and supporters, logging on to the online marketplace system first thing each morning in search of grocery bargains.

Arnold passed away in 2012, but if you were to ask him if he saw any contradiction between his enthusiasm as a Second Harvest market participant and his membership in the Socialist Party of America, we don't think he would. He, like many, sees American capitalism as the means by which the rich get richer. The Second Harvest market was just a really good way for him to get what he needed to feed the hungry in West Michigan. And it turns out markets are really good at that too. The Second Harvest auction market wasn't repugnant; it was badly misunderstood.

Trading Kidneys

Although there's no such thing as a living heart donor—you've got just one and without it you're dead—when Mother Nature was handing out kidneys, she gave us each a pair. A single well-functioning kidney is all you need to have a happy and healthy existence, with the second one serving as backup just in case. (Not so for lungs: everyone has a pair, but you function about half as well with only one.)

If, God forbid, you start having serious kidney problems—despite Nature's best intentions, when one goes they typically both go—there's a good chance you'll find yourself on a waiting list for a transplant. The list is long enough these days that the average wait time exceeds the average life expectancy of a dialysis patient. Which is a way of saying that people on the wait list frequently die.

As a potential recipient, you have only two paths to your new kidney, but either way, the donor has to match your blood type and pass a cross-matching test, which assesses whether a recipient's antibodies will reject the donor's kidney. The first path is to get a matched kidney from a recently deceased donor—but in 2014, there were only eleven thousand cadaver kidneys, while nearly forty thousand transplant candidates were added to the waiting list.[3]

There is another, better option: relatives and close friends may offer their backup kidney to a transplant candidate. That happened a few thousand times last year, and the outcomes from these donations are much better than those with a cadaver donor. (A donation can also come from an altruistic donor who offers a kidney to a stranger—including, apparently, a donation that resulted from a Tinder date. But these cases are so rare that they don't really matter to the population at large.)

Either way, the math does not look good: eleven thousand cadaver kidneys and a few thousand live donor kidneys fall far short of the seventy thousand recipients looking for a match. Each year, fifty thousand people in the United States alone just go without.

A few economists, including such eminent figures as Nobel laureate Gary Becker, have argued for organ sales as a means of resolving this shortfall. Becker lobbied for kidney markets as recently as January 2014 in a *Wall Street Journal* op-ed months before his death. He suggested a price of $15,000 for a kidney, $32,000 for a slice of liver (you can get away with just a slice because the liver regenerates once inside the recipient's body).[4]

You're probably thinking, "This is a sick idea." A market for kidneys may be efficient, but it's utterly disgusting—repugnant even. Arnold may have come to terms with bidding shares on peanut butter for his food bank, but most of us draw the line at using a market for allocating kidneys—although the *Journal*'s comments section was filled with supporters, and more than a few commenters offered up their own kidneys for a price, usually above Becker's suggested payment.

Becker, a truly brilliant economist, had a ready set of responses for these naysayers (which included, among others, Pope John Paul II and the Lutheran Church) and assured his readers that, with time, humanity would overcome its aversion to pricing body parts. After all, we accept the notion of impoverished coal miners in China risking their lives so the economy can keep chugging along, or watching linebackers wreck their brains on *Monday Night Football*. Lots of people wring their hands about such problems, but very few do anything about it: what we claim to care about diverges pretty significantly from what we reveal about our preferences through our actions.

But suppose we don't overcome our repugnance. Or suppose we could, but would rather not become that sort of society: no markets for Swedish classroom coat hooks and no markets for kidney donations, either. That's not who we want to be. As some of Becker's detractors point out, if we accept that a poor Indian can swap his kidney for cash, where does it all end? Cash for an eye, a leg, a heart?

If we won't let the market solve the problem, what's to be done for the thousands who die each year while waiting for a transplant?

Try to imagine that your brother goes into kidney failure. For months now he's had to go to a clinic a few times a week to have enormous needles poked into his arms, sitting for hours each time while his blood circulates through a dialysis machine. He's given a year to live. You'd be happy to give up a kidney to help him out. But when the doctors run the cross-match test, you find out you aren't a good fit as a donor.

That makes you a willing live donor with a needy but mismatched transplant candidate. There are lots of other mismatched donor-transplant pairs in the same position. If you turn out to be compatible with the transplant candidate in one of these other incompatible pairs, and his donor is, in turn, a match for your brother, there are gains from a kidney trade.

This kind of kidney swap has been taking place for decades but only haphazardly. A transplant surgeon with an incompatible live donor would need to call around to see if she could find another doctor who, by happenstance, also had a donor-recipient pair that was a suitable candidate for a swap. If she found a match, the two participating hospitals needed to arrange for two simultaneous transplants. At no point in the process can you force someone to give up an organ, so it was critical that both donors made their contribution at the same time, lest the second donor back out.

You might see why this ad hoc kidney barter system never really amounted to much, rarely getting past the teens in any given year: something like one or two donor-recipient exchanges for every ten thousand cases languishing on the transplant wait list.

The market lacked what market designer Al Roth calls thickness—the presence of enough "traders" at the kidney swap to make it worth searching for a partner. It's a self-fulfilling prophecy: since no one else is showing up to trade, it isn't worthwhile for anyone to participate. And as a result, there was no kidney exchange platform for traders to show up to in search of a match.

Roth and his fellow market designers set about revolutionizing the kidney transplant world in 2003 with an article that observed that kidney exchange bears a close resemblance to a problem that mathematical economists Lloyd Shapley (who you might recall from the Shapley-Gale matching algorithm) and Herbert Scarf examined in 1974. Shapley and Scarf originally used the metaphor of a house exchange to illustrate how their algorithm would work. You might like your own home, but perhaps there are other nearby houses you'd prefer. You'd be willing to give up your current residence for one of those. Some of your neighbors may similarly covet the homes of others. Maybe there are gains from trade. And if so, Shapley and Scarf wondered, how could you optimize the house exchange? Is there an algorithm that would convince everyone in the neighborhood to hand in an honest list of housing preferences and use this information to produce a set of housing swaps that made everyone better off (or at least no worse off)? And could it be designed to make the housing allocations stable (like the middle school dance), in the sense that, at the end, no pair of homeowners felt like they could do better by just switching their original homes "outside the market"?

It turns out that there is such an algorithm. Shapley and Scarf's landmark proof is presented rigorously in the language of math, but it has a straightforward and appealing intuition. For every home-owner, look at their list of housing preferences and "point" to the one at the top. Picture, if you will, the neighborhood with houses connected by arrows indicating which home each family would most like to move into. Shapley and Scarf proved that, among the arrows, there will always exist a closed loop, where each person in the circle of trades could move into his top-choice residence, while opening up his own home for the person "behind" him in the loop. They called this a top-trading cycle. In Shapley and Scarf's algorithm, you'd then pull all of the homes in this first cycle out of circulation, cross those houses off the lists of all remaining homeowners who haven't yet had a chance to make a swap, and repeat the process until there were no more home exchanges to be made.

Roth's transformative insight was that the kidney market bore a remarkable resemblance to this housing exchange. Each donor-recipient pair had a kidney on offer (the house, in Scarf and Shapley's example) and a person in need of a kidney (the family in search of another home). Each transplant candidate would "point" to his favored live donor kidney, and an algorithm could work through transplant cycles, with Donor A giving to Recipient B, Donor B giving to Recipient C, and so on, until it circled back to some Donor Z donating to Recipient A.

Roth and his colleagues published their idea in the May 2004 issue of the *Quarterly Journal of Economics* in an article titled "Kidney Exchange" and circulated it among contacts in the medical community.[5] Frank Delmonico, a surgeon who at the time was direc-tor of the New England Organ Bank, had lunch with Roth and his colleagues to talk about it. The New England Program for Kidney

Exchange arose from these conversations, as did a handful of other kidney clearinghouses around the country.

As with matching students to schools, the reality was inevitably more complicated than Scarf and Shapley's 1974 proof. You couldn't force someone to part with a kidney, so to make sure that no one broke the loop because of a change of—ahem—heart, all transplants in a cycle had to be done at once. It's a biomedical impossibility to execute a dozen transplants in tandem. In fact, it's impossible to do five, or even four.[6]

It is possible to string together much, much longer kidney chains if they start with an altruistic donation. This has made the rare breed of altruistic donors much more important to kidney exchanges today. Since there's no one back at the beginning loop waiting for payback, bioethicists have decided the transplants need not be simultaneous. If a donor somewhere in the chain backs out, the chain ends. But that is surprisingly rare, at least to economists who insist on thinking about people as coldly calculating and rational beings. One such chain led to the transfer of thirty-four kidneys—at hospitals around the United States—over the course of three months. There may be a lapse of months or occasionally even years between the receipt of a life-saving kidney and the recipient's donor making good on her promise to pay the good deed forward.

The initial algorithms only allowed for two-way exchanges, and even today cycles are limited to three: A gives to B, B gives to C, C gives to A—a set of swaps that still requires six adjacent operating rooms. (This might be enough: an analysis by Al Roth and his colleagues found that going as far as a three-way exchange may get you as much as 99 percent of the way toward the efficiency you'd get if you could allow for exchanges of any length.)

A decade after the article "Kidney Exchange" appeared, there were close to five hundred kidney swaps, a twenty-five-fold increase. Free-market zealots could point out (and often do) that this still falls very far short of closing the gap between kidney supply and demand, which selling kidneys would do. There are gains from kidney trade that aren't being realized by a sharecropper in rural India who could rise out of desperate poverty by giving up a redundant organ to a millionaire willing to shed half his bank account to get a single functioning kidney.

Then again, if there's one lesson you should take away from this book, it's that we've come to understand that in practice markets depart in many ways—some predictable, others less so—from textbook models of competition. If a global kidney market seems such a great idea in theory, it may be in part because it's never had the chance to fail.

Regardless, we may decide to maintain our disgust with cash-for-kidney exchanges. And if we do, we can be grateful that market designer Roth has invented another, more palatable means of getting kidneys to those who need them.

The Economics of Toxic Sludge

Larry Summers had been sticking his foot in his mouth long before some ill-chosen comments on gender differences in mathematical aptitude cost him his job as Harvard president in 2006. In 1991, Summers left his academic post at Harvard, where he'd taught since earning tenure in 1983 at the age of twenty-eight (that's very young—one of the youngest in Harvard's history), decamping to the World Bank to serve as chief economist, the first of a series of increasingly influential policy posts he's held in the decades since.

Early in his tenure at the bank, Summers signed his name to a memo that opened with the following tongue-in-cheek provocation: "Just between you and me, shouldn't the World Bank be encouraging MORE migration of the dirty industries to the LDCs [Least Developed Countries]?" He then went on to provide the impeccable economic arguments behind the promotion of exporting toxic industries and waste to poor countries, some of which provide an uncomfortable parallel to the ones we hear from organ market proponents: willingness to pay for extra years of life is lower in poor countries, so they should be willing to trade health and longevity in exchange for a bit of spending money from rich folk in Europe and America. When you're dirt poor, you're more concerned with food on the table than having your view obstructed by a power plant or garbage dump. A little pollution never hurt anyone, so undcrindustrialized nations shouldn't mind taking at least a bit of sludge and sulfur dioxide off rich countries' hands.

When the memo was inevitably leaked the following year, there was, predictably, a firestorm of criticism directed at Summers and his fellow economists—the absurdity of comparing the value of a rich versus a poor person's life, the focus on economic growth at all costs, the insensitivity of his tone. *The Economist*, a bastion of free-market journalism if ever there was one, ran a story entitled "Let Them Eat Pollution" about the memo that took Summers to task for his insensitivity. But then, like many free-market proponents, *The Economist* went on to give some credit to the basic argument, pointing out that "if clean growth means slower growth, as it sometimes will, its human cost will be lives blighted by a poverty that would otherwise have been mitigated." Economists and others also pointed out the insensitivity and paternalism of Summers's critics. What right do we, in the West, have to tell an impoverished Tanzanian whether he should want to trade a bit of his health or his country's nature for food or a TV if that's what he really wants?[7]

The memo was an indiscretion that, unfortunately for Summers, will likely live on in posterity. (The memo has its very own *Wikipedia* page.[8]) But the episode is telling: What would happen when Summers's theory met the real world? Would this be a case of market triumph or market failure?

Market logic can easily be turned on its head. In 2006, the *New York Times* described the aftermath of a cash-for-sludge transaction that, in a way, fits with Summers's logic. The *Times* recounts the story of a tanker filled with unidentified chemical waste that was to be deposited in Holland for safe disposal. But Amsterdam port authorities turned the ship away, owing to the extreme toxicity of its contents. So the tanker, itself of murky origins ("Greek-owned . . . flying a Panamanian flag and leased by the London branch of a Swiss trading corporation whose fiscal headquarters are in the Netherlands") journeyed on to the Ivory Coast where it found a willing partner in a local trash dealer named Tommy. The market at work![9]

Unfortunately, Tommy just dumped the lethal mix—"pitch black and with a heavy stench"—into the sewers of Abidjan, the

Ivory Coast's largest and most densely populated city. And this is how some city residents awoke one morning to the sight of a "stinking slick of black sludge." Local clinics saw cases of nausea, headaches, skin lesions, and nosebleeds by the hundreds.

Maybe, if they had had the chance, Abidjan residents would trade a headache or two for a week's wages, but no one ever saw a penny in recompense. Tommy kept the proceeds.

This little anecdote—hardly unique—might have tipped the free-market crowd at Cato and *The Economist* that Summers's idea had its problems. As we know from Arrow and Debreu, markets run best among willing and well-informed participants in places where the rules of exchange can be rigorously enforced. Abidjan isn't one of them. The dumping was in fact illegal, and in 2009 Trafigura, the Dutch company, was ultimately held responsible for the disaster and forced to pay thirty thousand Abidjan residents about $1,500 apiece. Some may see this as the market's vindication. We don't.

Consider, then, the story of an Illinois community's love affair with trash, chemical processing, strip clubs, and anything else that the rest of us don't want in our backyards. Why so? Because, as the *Wall Street Journal* reported in 2006, it had made the 250-person village of Sauget a "peculiar island of prosperity in the sea of urban economic blight across the Mississippi River from St. Louis. While the little towns around it are marked by crime, shuttered factories, burned-out buildings and trash-strewn streets, Sauget boasts clean parks, neat homes, and beautifully maintained roads." Per capita income in Sauget was around $19,000, supplemented by a whopping $28,000 in revenues from tax-paying businesses like a zinc smelter, toxic waste incinerator, and sewage treatment plant. Not many people are moving to Sauget—the population dropped below 160 by 2010—but for the citizens that remain, they've decided that $28,000 just about compensates for the porn, PCBs, and sewage.[10]

It's all well and good to then say, "Fine, we just need to make sure markets are set up to ensure everyone's fully informed of the trade-offs they're making, and no one is coerced into doing anything they wouldn't have chosen to do." In that world of perfect markets, every resident of Abidjan will be empowered to vote on whether a foreign multinational can buy the privilege of dumping sludge in his water supply in exchange for a five-figure fee. Then maybe Summers—along with Sauget's dwindling population—will be right.

But as a friend of ours likes to say, "I wish it rained beer. But it doesn't." We need to figure out how to adapt our models to reality, not the other way around.

Sharing

Economists aren't the only ones trying to recast the world in our model's image. If friction—informational, transactional, contractual—is all that stands between textbook economic models and the functioning of our real economy, then there is a vocal contingent out there ("there" being mostly Silicon Valley) that sees technology as the solution.

When viewed through the lens of market frictions, the much-hyped notion of the sharing economy can be seen as an effort to bring free-market salvation to bricks, mortars, and automobiles.

If you've ever tried to hail a taxi in San Francisco or rent a room in Washington, DC, you know the frictions of which we speak. The Bay Area's sprawl, combined with strict regulations on the cab and livery businesses, used to leave you at the mercy of the two thousand or so taxi medallion holders that covered San Francisco's 230 square miles. (By comparison, New York City has over seventeen thousand medallion holders taking pickups across Manhattan's thirty-four square miles.) Tight regulation didn't just make cabs hard to come by on a Friday night; it also gave them the upper hand in the driver-rider relationship. If the taxi dispatch said your ride would arrive in twenty minutes, and forty-five minutes later you were still waiting, what were you going to do about it?

The exasperating irony is that while you waited by the curb, you were very likely standing amid an endless supply of parked cars—idle capital, if you will. It just might be that if there were a frictionless way of calling all of their owners to see what they were up to, one of them would be willing to give you a lift in exchange for twenty dollars or so. And if only car owners knew there were twenty-dollar bills lining the Bay Area's suburban streets in the form of cab customers, lots would use their idle time to patrol the streets looking for rides instead of, say, dozing off in front of the TV.

This was the founding insight of the car service platform Uber. According to founder Garrett Camp (who had also created web discovery engine StumbleUpon), he was inspired by the fact that he couldn't get a cab in San Francisco's South Park neighborhood, even though he saw black town cars all over the area, presumably on their way to different appointments.

Now, idle car owners and their idle cars are being put to greater use in the service of those formerly at the mercy of taxi dispatchers. Taxi cartels worldwide are losing the fight against Uber and its sharing economy brethren, or face imminent disruption. And if you believe the Uber narrative, drivers and riders everywhere are rejoicing.

Something similar has happened in the market for short-term rentals as well. Washington is a city of transients: the steady churn of everyone from college kids to ex-CEOs cycling through government posts; employees of organizations like the World Bank, the US Agency for International Development, and Inter-American Development Bank (along with the dozens of consulting companies who serve them) who are forever coming or going from overseas postings; and political staffers who divide their time and loyalties between the nation's capital and their home constituencies.

That makes for a lot of idle real estate in Washington and a lot of short-term visitors of both the business and tourist variety. Again, a platform that matches visitors in need of a room to transient residents with empty ones could make a market that employs idle resources and creates a set of win-win real estate transactions. How do you know you're not rooming with an axe murderer? Well, his first twenty-six customers said he was a really nice guy. And you share three friends on Facebook! How do you know you're not renting your DC apartment to the Unabomber? He has twenty-six ratings too from prior rentals, and he left them all spotless. And there you have the Airbnb narrative.

All that's stopping Uber and Airbnb from realizing their dreams of a better, more efficient world are the villains in this laissez-faire fairy tale: the cab and hotel lobbies that profit from the old economy status quo (at the expense of the rest of us, as the Uber and Airbnb lobbies are quick to remind us) and their bureaucratic counterparts in government who are too lazy or rule-bound to care about doing what's right.

Let's start with what we can all agree on: the Uber app is awesome. Especially for the over-forty set who suffered under big taxi's reign for most of their adult lives, there's a head-shaking sense of amazement when you summon a cab with—literally—the touch of a button to pick you up from some godforsaken San Diego strip mall that happens to have the city's best sushi (the taxi dispatcher said it would be "at least an hour"). It's like having your own personal cab genie. (Just mention Uber to an iPhone-owning senior citizen, and you'll really see what we mean.) Airbnb is an epic leap forward when compared to the epic leap of faith involved in renting a room via its predecessors, the classified ads or Craigslist.

But let's not confuse a set of groundbreaking market innovations with the end of market frictions. Yes, there are entire websites devoted to Airbnb horror stories—the trashed homes, the tenant-turned-squatter. There's an equal number of angry rants directed at Uber. Neither of us rents our idle real estate assets when we're out of town and not because we're old-fashioned. We've also experienced market frictions of a more mundane variety. In writing this book we went to Washington to interview George Akerlof of market-for-lemons fame.

As a bit of add-on market research, one of us, Ray, decided to rent an apartment for the night via Airbnb. The renter's credentials were impeccable. He worked at an international organization and traveled a lot—hence the oft-vacant apartment. His place was described by past Airbnbers as neat, clean, well located. What could go wrong? Well, after arriving well past midnight courtesy of train delays, Ray found an unmade bed and suspiciously stained sheets. Whatever its shortcomings, you can be fairly sure that you won't be changing your own bedding at 2 a.m. when you're booked at the Marriott.

Did Ray leave an appropriately worded public review? No, actually. Because the host seemed like a nice guy, and anyway, what goes around comes around: you don't want to get known on Airbnb as Mr. Critical. (Ray did send a private communication to the host suggesting he wash his sheets more often.) So, yes, Airbnb is awesome: we've both used it a number of times since and mostly, but not always, successfully. But let's not kid ourselves by equating the advent of smart phones to market perfection.[11]

In saying that Airbnb and Uber have their problems, we're also not buying the taxi and hotel lobbies' line that they're merely protecting consumers from unreliable, unregulated, and sometimes outright dangerous conmen. Industry associations that argue for heavy government regulation do so for their own benefit not for some soft-hearted concern for their customers. After all, what better way to create a monopoly than to have it legislated into existence? Sometimes customers do see benefits: on balance, if we are ever in the market for a new kidney, we're glad that the transplant business is monopolized by certified transplant centers. But that's not why French cabbies are up in arms over Uber in Paris.

Taking a step back from the melodrama on both sides, let's consider some basic principles of free-market capitalism. As any serious entrepreneur in Silicon Valley or elsewhere will tell you, the last thing you want is for your own market to look like textbook competition. Because the textbook will also tell you that you're not really making that much money. Profits are competed away as you go toe-to-toe for customers.

Consider the case of Seven Minute Abs. In a scene from the Farrelly brothers' '90s classic, *There's Something About Mary*, Ted, played by a youthful Ben Stiller, picks up a hitchhiker on his way to Florida for one last chance at reconnecting with his high school crush, Mary. (This being a Farrelly brothers film, his first attempt at wooing Mary ended prematurely on prom night thanks to an unfortunate zipper malfunction.) The unnamed hitchhiker turns out to have an entrepreneurial bent and tells Ted of his plan to make a fortune off a "Seven Minute Abs" video, which would undercut the already best-selling "Eight Minute Abs." Ted bursts the hitchhiker's bubble by noting that he could easily be undercut by another would-be fitness mogul selling a "Six Minute Abs" video.

To build a profitable business, you need to create something that people want and then make sure there aren't any copycat competitors. The things that keep others out of Uber's sandbox, so to speak, aren't so different from the regulatory shenanigans that its predecessors resorted to. You try to erect what economists call barriers to entry, which are, almost by definition, market frictions. They're the strategies Uber and every other business employs to try to keep customers from choosing freely among competing options in the marketplace, whether by driving competitors out of business or finding ways of keeping customers from shopping around.

Sometimes, as we've learned from Uber in recent years, it can be a dirty business. They've been accused of misleading drivers on expected earnings (an information friction in the labor market) and calling then canceling rides from competing service Lyft (a friction in the market for rides), among other underhanded methods.

So yes, you want to build that game-changing app. But to get your $60 billion valuation, you need to create as many frictions as possible for everyone else. Although proponents of the sharing economy tout its ability to reduce market frictions, the only way they're going to make the kinds of profits they (and their investors) want is to create new ones. That's something they're not interested in talking about to the public at large, or to their representatives in government.

This leaves a bit of a paradox in the techno-utopian free-market narrative. A great entrepreneur will use technology to create a fantastic new market, then will use technology to set up market frictions to protect it. As entrepreneur and venture capitalist Peter Thiel wrote in the *Wall Street Journal*, "Competition Is for Losers."[12]

Don't get us wrong. We're not faulting the market makers of Silicon Valley nor begrudging them for the profits they've generated and captured. But we are trying to point out some of the inconsistencies between the claims of pristine competition espoused by free-market zealots in general and the practicalities of making markets work.

We've tried to communicate how a half century's worth of economic thought has better illuminated how Adam Smith's invisible hand works, and when it doesn't, and how economic theory has made markets work better and reach more deeply into our lives.

But our story is just as much about the many agents who, behind the scenes, set and enforce market rules, feed the market information, and bring buyer and seller together so we may come ever closer to the idealized markets of Arrow, Debreu, and Adam Smith. Without these market plumbers and engineers sticking their dirty (if invisible) fingers in all the right places to get the market to work just right, much more of the economy would look like George Akerlof's used car market. Free-market extremists take any evidence of active design as a violation of market logic per se, a view that's every bit as much of a pathology as the visceral reaction against anything involving money or market-like exchange.

Whether we're trying to allocate coat hooks, sell baseball player contracts, or just find a way home on a rainy Friday evening, we need to be clear about what we're looking for from our markets, and then think about how to go about designing them (and if necessary regulating them) so they do what we want them to do. Otherwise, we run the risk of thoughtlessly letting markets run amok or being paralyzed by a knee-jerk reaction to anything with a whiff of market exchange.

What happened with the problem of the Swedish coat hooks? Vlachos never did talk to anybody about his auction idea, so the students spent the winter competing for coat hooks. Then spring arrived, and the students no longer needed a place to hang their jackets. The next year, says Vlachos, the class moved to a longer hallway with more hooks, and the new class was left to deal with the problem.

9

HOW MARKETS SHAPE US

THE MAKING OF KING RAT

During the twenty weeks and six days of the 1960 Hollywood writers strike, James Clavell, a successful screenwriter, found himself with some time on his hands.

Clavell, an Australian-born Brit, had come to the United States in 1953 after a motorcycle accident left him with a lame leg, ending his military career. Through his wife, an aspiring actress, Clavell had become interested in film, and after working in distribution for a few years, he tried his hand at writing a script of his own. He quickly found considerable success in Hollywood, writing the screenplay for *The Fly* in 1958 and then the World War II epic *Five Gates to Hell* in 1959, before his career was interrupted by the walk-out. (After the strike was resolved, Clavell would go on to have a stellar career in both movies and television, most famously for the novel *Shogun* and the TV miniseries based on the book.)

During the strike, Clavell did what writers do: he wrote, producing his first novel, *King Rat*. It was an intensely personal story, based on Clavell's time as a POW in the notorious Changi prisoner-of-war camp near Singapore. It was a camp run by the Japanese military, which, you may recall from Chapter 1, was extremely harsh in its treatment of prisoners.

Clavell had been imprisoned in Changi in 1942, after being wounded by machine-gun fire while fighting the Japanese as an artillery officer. Those experiences became the basis for *King Rat*.[1]

The novel opens in early 1945. Peter Marlowe, a young British RAF flight lieutenant (based on Clavell), has been a POW since

1942. Marlowe comes to the attention of the King, an American corporal who has become the most successful trader and black marketer in Changi. The King is impressed by Marlowe's command of the local language (Malay), intelligence, and integrity and attempts to lure him into involvement with his black-market deals. This brings Marlowe to the attention of Lieutenant Robin Grey, the British provost marshal of the camp, who hopes to squelch the black-market trade and arrest the King. Grey aims to maintain military discipline among the prisoners—and to maintain his own position. As the son of a working-class family, Grey follows the rules for their own sake and exploits his position as provost marshal to gain a status otherwise unavailable to him in British society.

As American officer Lester Tenney, who we last met in Chapter 1, observed of Japanese camps, illicit markets allowed prisoners to manage the ebb and flow of calories and disease through trading. A prisoner might, for example, trade away a food ration on a day when he was too sick to keep it down, in exchange for a future meal. In a camp like Changi, with its ban on market exchange, the only way to survive (or at least improve the odds of it) was to work together as a small unit, where a sense of reciprocity in exchange would fill in for the market. If you happened into some good fortune, you'd share what you found. If you didn't share (and were found out), you would be expelled from your "tribe"—left to suffer by yourself. Such was the importance of the group that, when two prisoners are threatened by their colonel with banishment from their regiment, Clavell writes, "to get shipped out would mean that they would not exist to their cobbers [buddies], and without their cobbers, they'd die."

Only one man in Changi didn't need a unit or partner: Corporal King. "Nobody gives me nothing. . . . What I have is mine and I made it," the King tells Marlowe. The King's means of survival was the market, and his talent for trading made him a major power in the closed society of the POW camp. He traded with Korean guards, local Malay villagers, and other prisoners for food, clothing, information, and what few luxuries were available to keep himself and his fellow American prisoners (who served as the King's lackeys) alive. Senior officers came to him for help in selling their valuables—including a Montblanc fountain pen and an Oyster Royal Rolex watch—to buy what they needed to survive.

Marlowe is put off by the King, whose rough—and, as Clavell makes clear, very American—manners are at odds with Marlowe's British upper-class ideals. As Marlowe tells the King, "Marlowes aren't tradesmen. It just isn't done, old boy." But he nonetheless succumbs, ultimately, to the temptation of the King and the market.

After the camp is liberated at the end of the war, the King is taken away by the military police to be tried for his black-market activities. The prisoners depart, abandoning the rats they had resorted to breeding for food in their cages. The final scene shows the rats fighting and eating one another, with the final survivor being the "king of the rats."[2]

And that image, which, together with the King's success as a trader helped give the book its title, illustrates the complicated relationship that *King Rat* has with the idea of the market—and maybe the fraught relationship we all have.

Although markets often help keep people alive and better off than they might be otherwise (which is the key to the King's success), they also provide the King with outsized rewards, leading to inequitable and seemingly unfair results. He is better fed, better dressed, and wields far more power than nearly anyone else at Changi. Markets also disrupt traditional social order, despite Lieutenant Grey's best efforts to maintain it. The market can be a source of turmoil that, whatever its virtues, can be tough to live through.

Markets can also transform who we are. They can make us behave in ways that—in contrast to the beauty of the metaphor of the invisible hand—make us all worse off (part of the reason why others so disliked the King). And competition itself, part of the lifeblood of how markets work, not only drives away profits but can drive out concerns of morality and compassion that may come to be seen as an unaffordable indulgence.

Markets Can Make Us Selfish

In 1977, Stanford psychologist Lee Ross and some colleagues published a landmark article on attribution theory, which is "concerned with the attempts of ordinary people to understand the causes of the events they witness. It deals with the 'naïve psychology' of the 'man in the street' as he interprets his own behaviors and the actions of others." Ross's central question was, How do we ordinary people judge why others appear selfish or generous, cheerful or grumpy, docile or aggressive? Ross notes at the outset that the "exploration of the [ordinary person's] shortcomings must start with his general tendency to overestimate the importance of personal . . . factors relative to environmental influences."[3]

In other words, we tend to excessively attribute blame and give credit to the *person* rather than his or her *situation*. If a waiter is curt we assume it's because he's ornery instead of observing that he's dealing with the lunchtime rush (or responding to your own rudeness at his delay in taking your order). If a hedge fund manager earns 30 percent on returns, we assume she's a genius, when in fact she almost certainly just got lucky.[4]

This failure in judgment was so central to how we judge others that Ross termed it the fundamental attribution error, and it serves as a potent illustration of the power of circumstance rather than individual volition in explaining the choices we make.

A 2004 study by Ross and a pair of coauthors provides some intriguing insights into how "the market" affects how we behave. The study focused on a game called the prisoners' dilemma, a staple of game theory, which presents the following quandary to a pair of criminals. Both have been arrested, and the cops are trying to elicit a confession from each suspect separately, offering them both the same deal: if one testifies against the other while the other remains silent, the confessor goes free and the silent one suffers the full force of the law, let's say ten years in jail. If both remain silent, the cops don't have much on them, so they each receive much lighter sentences, only a few months. Finally, if each betrays the other, the cops will have their charges, but also go easy on them for cooperating; both receive a yearlong sentence. Do you betray your partner or cooperate with her and remain silent, even though she won't know you're cooperating when she makes her decision?[5]

If each prisoner cares only about serving the least amount of jail time, the "rational" choice leads both players to confession and betrayal because you get less prison time that way *regardless* of what the other suspect chooses to do. If the other prisoner confesses, you get a year instead of a decade of jail time by confessing; if the other prisoner stays silent, you can still save yourself a few months in prison (and screw your partner over) by giving a confession and going free. No matter what the other does, each partner is best off confessing. The dilemma is that both *could* be best off if only they'd both stay quiet. The cruel genius of the prisoners' dilemma is that selfish motivations undermine the prisoners' common good.

In Ross et al.'s version of the prisoner's dilemma, instead of prison time, pairs of lab subjects earn money based on whether they cooperate or defect. But as with the classic formulation, subjects can always increase their earnings by defecting, even though members of a pair would be better off if only they'd both cooperate.

Ross's innovation was to reframe the prisoners' dilemma as either the Wall Street game or the community game. The payoffs—and so the incentives to defect or cooperate—were *identical*. All that differed was that subjects were cued to think they were either Wall Street traders or community builders. Outside observers of the experiment predicted that the defection rates would be virtually identical for both versions of the game.[6]

But the framing effect was shockingly large. Those randomly assigned to play the Wall Street game defected nearly 70 percent of the time, more than twice as often as those in the community game. Ross and his colleagues also recorded what participants expected their partners would do, and in the Wall Street game, subjects defected in large part because they expected their partners were about to do the same.

More than we ever imagined, the situation trumped the individual.

We may not even realize it, but "the market" makes us selfish in such a way that undermines the common good. Wall Street participants work harder to maximize their earnings, but in doing so, they end up poorer than the community players. This irony shows how the market, by undermining our concern for others and beliefs in the intentions of others, can end up shrinking rather than growing the economic pie.

Competition Can Make Us Unethical

In a 2004 essay, Harvard economist Andrei Shleifer speculated that competitive markets—the holy grail of free marketers—have the potential to make us not just selfish but downright unethical. As his point of departure, Shleifer presumes that ethical conduct is what economists call a normal good—something we consume more of as we get richer. (Ramen noodles, perennial staple of poor college students, are a classic example of an inferior good, where you consume less of it once you can afford not to.)[7]

The owners of a company with fat profit margins and an unassailable position in the marketplace—Google or Microsoft, for example—can afford to be honest and charitable. But business owners in the cutthroat business of textile production in Bangladesh, say, might not have this luxury. As competition for contracts drives prices ever lower, there's inevitably the temptation to cut corners on worker or product safety just to make a living.

Shleifer also discusses a number of morally fraught cases where a practice is viewed as repugnant but, at least under some circumstances, has the potential to make the community economically better off. Competition might drive some firms to employ child labor—which, for a while at least, could make those families richer than if they educated their kids. But it would also be easy to get stuck in the habit of using child labor long after its alleged efficiency benefits have been eclipsed by the higher returns on education. The same could be said of banning usury: lending money and collecting interest used to be considered unethical despite serving as the basis of efficient capital markets. Medieval clerics would be horrified by our casual use of interest to make the wheels of finance turn, but of course interest is the lifeblood of modern finance.

But Shleifer's main point is that, under certain circumstances, "competition increases censured conduct." Market competition, which in their classic paper Arrow and Debreu showed would create the most efficient of all possible worlds, might actually change who we are and in ways we probably don't like. It can make us pay bribes, shirk on expenditures that would protect workers from sickness or death, and cut corners on product quality that may eventually do the same to our customers. Competitive markets make us bad people.

None of this is good news if markets are infiltrating ever more corners of our lives.

Shleifer is, however, quick to counter his own arguments. He points out that competition might get rid of many "costly" indulgences on the part of businesses that we'd view as both unethical *and* inefficient. For example, a company that will only employ white workers will be at a disadvantage relative to a colorblind one that hires well-qualified black applicants. Market pressures might force a racist business owner to reconsider his principles. And if, despite their shortcomings, competitive markets tend to make society richer overall, they'll soon lead to the happier state of affairs where we can indulge our preferences for honest, upright living.

$$$

When we began our discussion of markets in Chapter 1, with R. A. Radford in Stalag VII-A, they seemed very much a force for good. Markets helped POWs survive. They help people get what they want. But remember the book's central premise: our present and future are built upon the skeleton of yesterday and today's economic theory, ideas that originally appeared in the pages of esoteric academic journals. When loosed upon the world, those theories have contributed to the growth of new kinds of markets and market-like mechanisms that now define much of how we interact. To a large extent, though, we haven't really noticed the creep of markets into every area of our lives.

Taken together, the evidence about how markets can affect our behavior combined with the new ways that markets are impinging on our lives should make the rest of us at least a bit uneasy about our future.

We've deliberately stayed out of the business of proposing regulations. Nor have we said anything about how, absent regulation, participants *should* conduct themselves in market transactions. But these are clearly relevant issues.

We're not going to propose an optimal set of regulations, nor will we end with a sermon on market ethics. But if we're going to have a thoughtful discussion about markets and the role that market logic plays in our lives, we have to have a deeper conversation about what problem regulation is trying to solve—that is, what markets are and aren't doing well. None of the market innovations that have appeared since World War II have changed the fact that markets sometimes need a bit of help and oversight to perform their miracles of efficiency. But we need to better understand these innovations to have a conversation about what's wrong with today's markets.

When it distributes food to POWs, the market is a marvelous social good; when it tries to price a human life, it often wreaks havoc. To paraphrase Nobel laureate (and free-market critic) Joseph Stiglitz, sometimes we can't see the invisible hand of the market working not because it's invisible, but because it isn't there at all.

The tougher cases are where the market *does* do its job of creating a more efficient society, but in doing so creates winners and losers and perhaps even affects whether we think life is a community game or a Wall Street competition. How high a price are we willing to pay for a more efficient world? It's not up to us (or the architects of the new market economy) to say.

It's up to you.

ACKNOWLEDGMENTS

We'd like to start by thanking Jay Mandel, our agent, and his colleagues at William Morris Endeavor Entertainment. Jay was incredibly helpful in seeing the value in our idea and helping us give it shape in the proposal.

We'd also like to thank Benjamin Adams, our editor, and his colleagues at PublicAffairs, including Melissa Veronesi, our project manager, Kate Mueller, our copyeditor (who saved us from more than one embarrassing mistake), and Tony Forde, our publicist. We'd also like to thank Iain Campbell, our publisher in the United Kingdom, and his team at John Murray.

We'd like to thank the following people who read the manuscript, or parts of it, or who graciously agreed to talk with us about ideas in the book: George Akerlof, Kenneth Arrow, Pierre Azoulay, Seth Dicthick, Frank Dobbin, Ben Edelman, Teppo Felin, Ronald Findlay, Todd Fitch, Margo Beth Fleming, Walter Frick, Joshua Gans, Ed Glaeser, Andrei Hagiu, Matthew Kahn, Judd Kessler, Barbara Kiviat, Scott Kominers, Ilyana Kuziemko, Kevin Li, Roger Martin, Eric Maskin, Dan McGinn, Ben Olken, Joel Podolny, Jeff Pontiff, Canice Prendergast, Paul Romer, Marc Rysman, Peng Shi, Paolo Siconolfi, Paulo Soumaini, Michael Spence, Kendall Sullivan, Morgan Sword, Steve Tadelis, Jonas Vlachos, Ania Wieckowski, and Feng Zhu.

Finally, we'd like to thank our families for putting up with our new all-consuming "hobby" of book writing. You didn't sign up for this, and we appreciate your patience, good humor, and support.

NOTES

Preface

1. We've been looking for this book for ages. If you know what it is, tell us.

Chapter 1. Why People Love Markets

1. R. A. Radford, "The Economic Organisation of a P.O.W. Camp," *Economica* 12, no. 48 (November 1945): 189–201. See also Radford's obituary in the *Washington Post*: http://www.washingtonpost.com/wp-dyn/content/article /2006/11/13/AR2006111301396.html.

2. Anything can serve as a medium of exchange, as long as it's scarce and we all agree on its worth, such as gold, pieces of counterfeit-proof paper, cigarettes, or computer passkeys. For a brief time in 2013, boxes of Tide detergent were the currency of choice among drug dealers in the southwestern United States. See Ben Paynter, "Suds for Drugs," *New York* magazine, January 6, 2013.

3. You can read Murphy's account at http://www.moosburg.org/info/stalag /murphyeng.html.

4. William Bole, "Trading Places: In POW Camps, Officers Could Impede Survival," *Boston College Magazine*, 2012, http://bcm.bc.edu/issues/fall_2012 /inquiring_minds/trading-places.html#sthash.afW3MYc9.dpuf.

5. Clifford G. Holderness and Jeffrey Pontiff, "Hierarchies and the Survival of POWs during WWII," *Management Science* (2012).

6. To give just a few examples, Google's AdWords algorithm (which decides who gets paid search listings and how much they pay) was designed by Berkeley economist Hal Varian. Amazon poached its chief economist, Pat Bajari, from the University of Minnesota. Uber, Pandora, Airbnb, and others have all hired PhD economists to act as, in the words of *The Economist*, Silicon Valley's "market shapers," economists who tinker with the rules and algorithms that govern their sites.

7. "Meet the Market Makers," *The Economist*, January 8, 2015, http://www .economist.com/news/finance-and-economics/21638152-new-breed-high-tech -economist-helping-firms-crack-new-markets-meet.

8. This is at least acknowledged by more thoughtful market proponents. In a 1970 *New York Times* essay, Milton Friedman himself famously made the case for the necessary inefficiencies of democracy.

Chapter 2. The Scientific Aspirations of Economists, and Why They Matter

1. Kieran Healy, "Fuck Nuance," working paper, Duke University, August 2015.

2. Gérard Debreu, "The Mathematization of Economic Theory," *American Economic Review* 81, no. 1 (March 1991): 1–7.

3. Marion Fourcade, Etienne Ollion, and YannAlgan. "The Superiority of Economists," *Journal of Economic Perspectives* 29, no. 1 (2015): 89–114.

4. Smith did consider situations where selfish interests worked against the greater good. He pointed out, for example, that monopolists—often government sanctioned in Smith's day—would charge prices that were "too high" relative to what the invisible hand would have dictated. As Smith put it, "The monopolists, by keeping the market constantly understocked, by never fully supplying the effectual demand, sell their commodities much above the natural [market] price, and raise their emoluments, whether they consist in wages or profit, greatly above their natural rate."

5. History has not been kind to many of Pareto's theories. In a mostly adoring profile in the *Quarterly Journal of Economics* in 1949, Joseph Schumpeter still called Pareto's work "far from faultless," before describing his theory of money as "inferior" and noting that Pareto's "theory of monopoly cannot, I believe, be salvaged by even the most generous interpretation."

6. Pareto, who in his earlier life often railed against antimarket policies like import tariffs, was far from a blind adherent to free-market ideology. In fact, in his *Manuele di economia politica*, Pareto presents underinvestment in railroads as a clear violation of Pareto optimality that would occur if infrastructure construction were left in the hands of private business.

7. Marx wasn't implying that customer value or preferences were irrelevant. His was a model where price was an outcome that would, in market equilibrium, be defined by labor inputs. As Etsy sellers can attest, Marx's model doesn't seem to pan out in reality.

8. One notable exception who continues to have an outsized influence was Friedrich Hayek, an Austrian-born economist who took up a post at the London School of Economics in 1931. Hayek was as much a social theorist and political philosopher as an economist. Despite his reliance on narrative argument over mathematical proof, he won the Nobel Prize, with Gunnar Myrdal, in 1974, for his "penetrating analysis of the interdependence of economic, social and institutional phenomena." Hayek died in 1992. Others who also followed in the "more words than math" school include Albert Hirschman and Arthur Lewis.

9. Joseph Schumpeter, *Theory of Economic Development* (Cambridge, MA: Harvard University Press, 1949).

10. Mathematics can also obfuscate and serve as a smokescreen for political or ideological agendas. This debate in economics came to the fore in 2015 with the publication of an article by the great macroeconomist Paul Romer, who accused a number of celebrated economists (including two Nobel

laureates, one of them Romer's thesis supervisor) of engaging in "mathiness"—using opaque mathematics to support a free-market agenda. Paul Romer, "Mathiness in the Theory of Economic Growth," *American Economic Review: Papers & Proceedings* 105, no. 5 (2015): 89–93.

11. The foundation moved to the University of Chicago in 1939 and then to Yale in 1955, where it remains today.

12. That article and other relevant reviews are available in the sixtieth anniversary edition of the original, published by Princeton University Press in 2004.

13. Oskar Morgenstern, "The Cold War Is Cold Poker," *New York Times*, February 5, 1961, quoted in James McManus, *Cowboys Full: The Story of Poker* (New York: Farrar, Straus and Giroux, 2009), 225.

14. For more on these trends, see Till Düppe and E. Roy Weintraub, *Finding Equilibrium: Arrow, Debreu, McKenzie, and the Problem of Scientific Credit* (Princeton, NJ: Princeton University Press, 2014).

15. Available at http://www.nobelprize.org/nobel_prizes/economic-sciences/laureates/1970/.

16. Among other feats, Samuelson also revolutionized publishing, as textbook publishers recognized the same fact and sought to recreate that magic in a bottle by paying young economics professors ungodly sums of money to try to unseat Samuelson's *Economics*.

17. Sylvia Nasar, "A Hard Act to Follow? Here Goes," *New York Times*, March 14, 1995, http://www.nytimes.com/1995/03/14/business/a-hard-act-to-follow-here-goes.html; Michael E. Weinstein, "Paul Samuelson, Economist, Dies at 94," *New York Times*, December 13, 2009, http://www.nytimes.com/2009/12/14/business/economy/14samuelson.html?_r=0.

18. Kenneth J. Arrow and Gérard Debreu, "Existence of an Equilibrium for a Competitive Economy," *Econometrica* 22, no. 3 (July 1954): 265–290.

19. Arrow is the only member of the lunch group still alive and is perhaps too modest to recall it. But at least one of Arrow's contemporaries swears to its veracity, having heard it directly from one of the protagonists in the 1970s. A variant on this story involves gray whale breeding instead of Australian aboriginals, and junior faculty rather than senior colleagues, but is otherwise the same. This version seems to have originated with Eric Maskin, who told us he heard the story while still a graduate student but cannot attest to its veracity.

20. Or, more accurately, only in very limited and circumscribed situations. The University of Pennsylvania's Wharton School of Business uses the general equilibrium framework in running student course selection. The system was designed and implemented by two economists, Wharton's Judd Kessler and the University of Chicago's Eric Budish.

21. Joseph Stiglitz, "Information and the Change in the Paradigm in Economics," Nobel Prize lecture, December 8, 2001.

22. Stiglitz is alluding to state-contingent claims, which were developed as part of the general equilibrium theory to take account of the fact that market

transactions unfold over time. A state-contingent claim (or Arrow-Debreu security) pays off when a certain "state" of the world occurs. For example, you could, in theory, design an asset that pays a dollar if Hillary Clinton is elected president *and* there's an earthquake in Japan in 2018 *and* the polar ice caps melt by 2050, and nothing otherwise. More practically, state-contingent models created a framework for thinking about the price of an apple in New York in September versus an apple in Paris in June. These ideas have had enormous practical application in helping lay the groundwork for modern finance theory.

23. Nicholson Baker's books are the exception that proves the rule.

24. There are many, many others who contributed to the development of economics over this period who we do not mention here but are well worth knowing about: go read Robert L. Heilbroner's *The Worldly Philosophers: The Lives, Times, and Ideas of the Great Economic Thinkers* (New York: Simon & Schuster, 1995; first published 1953), if you're interested, for a start.

Chapter 3. How One Bad Lemon Ruins the Market

1. Personal communications.

2. For a great take on the what the web means to knowledge, see all of David Weinberger's work, but especially *Small Pieces Loosely Joined: A Unified Theory of the Web* (New York: Basic Books, 2002).

3. Jim Snider and Terra Ziporyn, *Future Shop: How Future Technologies Will Change the Way We Shop & What We Buy* (New York: St. Martin's Press, 1992); Jonathan Kirsch, "Consumer Manifesto: Power to the Buyer," book review, Special to the Times, *Los Angeles Times*, February 12, 1992, http://articles .latimes.com/1992-02-12/news/vw-1482_1_future-shop; academic review by E. Scott Maynes, *Review of Industrial Organization* 8, no. 5 (October 1993): 639–643.

4. Podolny had made his academic name trying to understand the role that status played as a solution to such market uncertainty. Status, which is a function of who and what you associate with, is a notion that has traditionally been more the domain of sociologists than economists, and one that we will not delve into in any detail in this book.

5. George Akerlof, "The Market for 'Lemons': Quality Uncertainty and the Market Mechanism," *Quarterly Journal of Economics* 84, no. 3 (1970): 488–500.

6. In a roundabout way, thinking about business cycles and unemployment is what led Akerlof to the market for used cars in particular as a setting for his lemons model. The market forces that drive unemployment to zero in standard models should also dampen the ups and downs of used car sales: if a used car is anywhere near substitutable for a new one, then as new car demand (and prices) go up during booms, at least some buyers should switch to shopping for a used one, thus tamping down new car demand. But in reality, the car market is highly cyclical. Understand the feast and famine market for cars, and perhaps we would be one step closer to explaining the economy's broader ups and downs. Economists could no better make sense of this fact than they could explain recessions more generally.

Akerlof never got around to tying his lemons model back to the cyclicality of new car sales that was his original motivation. This was left to Frederick Mishkin, who in 1976 explained why consumers avoid buying hard-to-unload assets like cars during recessions. Intuitively, it's because they might need money to, say, pay the rent or feed their family. So better to have cash in the bank than a car in the driveway. You don't worry as much during a boom when risk of unemployment is low. Where does the lemons argument come in? Because it causes the car market to unravel, making it difficult to convert a vehicle into cash.

7. The Nobel Committee did eventually award a prize to a trio of economists for their work on search theory and unemployment, nine years after Akerlof received his prize. Furthermore, Akerlof himself deployed search models in a 1985 paper that aimed to explain persistent discrimination in market economies in a way that he *did* find to be satisfactory. This work hasn't had the same lasting influence on the field of economics: Akerlof's model of discrimination has received under one hundred citations on Google Scholar, as compared to nearly seventeen thousand for the market for lemons.

8. They've come a long way but certainly haven't solved the problem. At the time of writing, the Chinese company Alibaba, which had just had its IPO on the New York Stock Exchange, saw its stock price drop by about a third. Why? Its main business, Taobao, was China's answer to eBay. And it was uncovered shortly after its listing in New York that an enormous fraction of its listings were counterfeits.

9. yvonne9903, "How to Spot Fake Tiffany Jewelry," eBay, September 11, 2011, http://www.ebay.com/gds/How-To-Spot-Fake-Tiffany-Jewelry-/10000000001241859/g.html, last visited February 18, 2014.

10. Beyond the inability to physically inspect goods for sale, internet commerce also just seems to bring out the worst in us all. Social psychologists and negotiations experts have run experiments proving what you probably already know intuitively: there is more trust and honesty in face-to-face interactions than in online ones. See, for example, Charles E. Naquin and Gaylen D. Paulson, "Online Bargaining and Interpersonal Trust," *Journal of Applied Psychology* 88, no. 1 (2003): 113.

11. We've simplified the situation for ease of exposition here. The participants, being MBA students, were familiar with terms like "tender offer" and "tender in cash." We will not presume any such background on the part of the reader.

12. We thank Ilyana Kuziemko for suggesting this example.

Chapter 4. The Power of Signals in a World of Cheap Talk

1. Scott Glover, "A Marked Man from Tattoo to Taps," *Los Angeles Times*, October 18, 1997, http://articles.latimes.com/1997/oct/18/news/mn-44041.

2. It's not entirely correct to say that mere words carry no weight. Imagine, for example, two business partners whose interests are reasonably well aligned. Both parties have an incentive to be honest. If one tells the other,

"We're almost out of ketchup—please order some more," the other has every reason to believe that ketchup inventories are in fact dangerously low. The more that the two partners' interests overlap, the easier it is for them to take the other at his word. These sorts of issues were first examined in a 1982 paper by game theorists Vince Crawford and Joel Sobel, though the term "cheap talk" didn't find its way into common use in economics until some years later. See Vincent P. Crawford and Joel Sobel, "Strategic Information Transmission," *Econometrica* 50, no. 6 (1982): 1431–1451.

3. A. Michael Spence, "Signaling in Retrospect and the Informational Structure of Markets," Prize Lecture, December 8, 2001, http://www.nobel prize.org/nobel_prizes/economic-sciences/laureates/2001/spence-lecture .html.

4. A pessimistic view is that every worker is either one or the other. As the scientific management pioneer Frederick Taylor once put it: "Hardly a competent workman can be found who does not devote a considerable amount of time to studying just how slowly he can work and still convince his employer that he is going at a good pace."

5. Eli Berman, "Sect, Subsidy, and Sacrifice: An Economist's View of Ultra-Orthodox Jews," *Quarterly Journal of Economics* 115, no. 3 (2000).

6. Diego Gambetta, *Codes of the Underworld: How Criminals Communicate* (Princeton, NJ: Princeton University Press, 2009).

7. "Maine Attorney General Stops Telemarketing of Dubious Baldness, Psoriasis, and Weight-Loss Products," Quackwatch, November 2003, http:// www.quackwatch.org/02ConsumerProtection/AG/ME/folliguard.html.

8. "Return to Spender," Snopes.com, last updated April 25, 2011, http:// www.snopes.com/business/consumer/nordstrom.asp.

9. Paul Milgrom and John Roberts, "Price and Advertising Signals Product Quality," *Journal of Political Economy* 94, no. 4 (1986): 796–821.

10. This fits with what economists call a pooling equilibrium where all sellers are forced to adopt the signal, and the consequences of nonadoption are being singled out as a truly infirm enterprise that can't even afford to burn a few million bucks on a thirty-second ad spot.

11. Dashiell Bennett, "8 Dot-Coms That Spent Millions on Super Bowl Ads and No Longer Exist," *Business Insider*, February 2, 2011, http://www.business insider.com/8-dot-com-super-bowl-advertisers-that-no-longer-exist-2011-2; Emily Steel, "Newcomers Buy Ad Time at the Super Bowl," *New York Times*, January 30, 2015, http://www.nytimes.com/2015/01/31/business/media /newcomers-buy-ad-time-at-the-super-bowl.html?_r=0.

12. There is a high correlation between companies' charitable expenditures and their advertising budgets. See Ray Fisman, Geoffrey Heal, and Vinay B. Nair, "A Model of Corporate Philanthropy," working paper, Columbia Business School, 2007.

13. Interestingly, in the months after Hurricane Katrina made landfall in August 2005, there was a big boost in sales probability and price from Giving Works for all eBay sellers, young and old. So, when a national spotlight shines

on particular causes, it may be possible to make money off being charitable. We'd conjecture that probably a lot of shady sellers put up charitable listings at times like this.

14. It's not just because customers are reluctant to complain about a seller who is donating money from their purchase price to charity; philanthropically inclined sellers also have about half as many unresolved disputes on their *noncharity* listings.

15. Akerlof never imagined that all consumers were aware of their own ignorance; for him the lemons model was merely a next step in a larger agenda. In *Phishing for Phools: The Economics of Manipulation and Deception* (Princeton, NJ: Princeton University Press, 2015), Akerlof and his coauthor Robert Shiller lay out a theory of markets where there are economic agents who are unaware of their ignorance (and hence buy too many subprime mortgages) or lack self-control (and eat too much ice cream). Such problems lead to what they call a "phishing equilibrium" where weak or ignorant consumers ("phools") are taken advantage of by exploitative firms.

Chapter 5. Building an Auction for Everything

1. Before the posting system, there was no agreed-upon mechanism for dealing with players who wanted to migrate between the two leagues while under contract. The legendary forkballer Hideo Nomo was the first to make waves when he "retired" from baseball while still under contract with the Kintetsu Buffalos in January 1995, only to reappear at spring training with the LA Dodgers a few months later. Under the terms of his retirement, Nomo was prohibited from playing for other teams. His agent argued the contract applied only to teams in Japan. Kintetsu management felt he'd unfairly exploited a legal loophole. Japanese fans called him a traitor. Nippon League owners closed the loophole after that, claiming that the prohibition following retirement applied worldwide. This issue came to a head when American Alfonso Soriano, fed up with the intensity of the practice regime in Japan, attempted to leave the Hiroshima Toyo Carp to return to American baseball. Carp executives notified American teams that they were prohibited from negotiating with Soriano. The matter came to MLB commissioner Bud Selig, who sided with Soriano. At that point, though, it was clear that the two leagues needed a mutual agreement, which led to the negotiation of the posting system.

2. Michael Silverman, "Why $51,111,111.11? John Henry Explains," *Boston Herald*, December 15, 2006, http://www.bostonherald.com/sports/red_sox _mlb/clubhouse_insider/2006/12/why_5111111111_john_henry_explains.

3. David Lucking-Reiley, "Vickrey Auctions in Practice: From Nineteenth-Century Philately to Twenty-First-Century E-Commerce," *Journal of Economic Perspectives* 14, no. 3 (2000): 183–192. This section draws on this *JEP* article by Lucking-Reiley, now a principal scientist at the online music site Pandora. At the time he wrote the article, Lucking-Reiley was teaching auction theory at Vanderbilt University and working on an overview article on real-world

applications of Vickrey auctions. He came across a stamp dealer whose website described the mechanism he used in selling lots via online bidding. It was a Vickrey auction. Lucking-Reiley contacted the dealer by e-mail asking why he used a second-price auction format and was told that stamp dealers had been doing sales that way for longer than he could remember. Lucking-Reiley's subsequent investigations into the origins of Vickrey auctions among stamp dealers are contained in his *JEP* article.

4. Findlay, Vickrey's friend for well over a decade, similarly knew very little of his family background. All he could recall was that the desk that Vickrey used (which was bequeathed to Findlay) had been given to Vickrey's father for his work on famine relief. So studying the science of scarcity ran in the family.

5. William Vickrey, *Public Economics: Selected Papers from William Vickrey*, eds. Richard Arnott et al. (New York: Cambridge University Press, 1997), 7; interview with Findlay.

6. Congestion pricing is related to Uber's surge pricing, where prices go up when there are fewer cars or more people looking for a ride. But the rationale is a bit different. Vickrey was focused on preventing the negative externalities that occur when a system is overloaded by too many customers. Uber just wants to reequilibrate supply and demand in real time to let markets clear—to make sure supply meets demand—by the minute.

7. A classic result in auction theory, the Revenue Equivalence Theorem, shows that, with appropriate assumptions on buyer and seller attributes like risk preferences, first- and second-price auctions can be expected to generate the same revenues for the seller, on average. Essentially, bidders in a first-price auction will shave their bids by "just enough" so that on average the amount paid to the seller is about the same. Sometimes it'll be higher under a second-price auction, sometimes lower, but over time it'll even out such that the choice between the two is, in theory, irrelevant.

8. This is a major issue in the design of broadband auctions, which sell internet bandwidth to cable and internet companies. In such scenarios it's useful for a single party to assemble a bundle of spectrum rights because, for example, it's only valuable to have the rights to a given spectrum band in Trenton if you also get it in nearby Newark. The FCC auction that was in progress at the time of writing, which we allude to at the end of the chapter, uses a much more complicated Vickrey-like auction, conducted across multiple rounds of sealed bids, to deal with this and other real-world complications. But the auction's basic machinery still builds off Vickrey's fundamental insight on second-bid auctions.

9. "In the Great Web Bazaar," *The Economist*, February 24, 2000, http://www.economist.com/node/285614; Robert Hall, *Digital Dealing: How E-Markets Are Transforming the Economy* (New York: W. W. Norton, 2002).

10. Recall in Chapter 4 that we looked at how eBay sellers experimented with bundling listings with charitable donations.

11. Economists have come up with a number of explanations for this end-of-auction "sniping." For example, a paper by Alvin Roth and Axel Ockenfels

argues that bidders learn about what an item is worth during the bidding process. The "snipers" wait to see how others value a listing before swooping in at the last moment to put in a slightly higher bid. Alvin E. Roth and Axel Ockenfels, "Last-Minute Bidding and the Rules for Ending Second-Price Auctions: Evidence from eBay and Amazon Auctions on the Internet," *American Economic Review* 92, no. 4 (2002): 1093–1103.

12. On this particular day, each Black and Silver 16 GB iPod was listed by a different seller, which accounts for much of the variability in prices for the same color and version of an iPod. You'll naturally pay more to buy from a top-rated merchant than someone new to the site. The eBay researchers only compared the outcomes of identical items listed by the same seller, to ensure that it wasn't the difference in the trustworthiness of sellers who tend to list auctions versus those that use posted prices. Such seller experiments are relatively rare, but the fact that at any given time there are hundreds of millions of eBay sales-in-progress means that there were still millions of seller experiments to explore in the data.

13. Lawrence M. Ausubel and Paul Milgrom, "The Lovely but Lonely Vickrey Auction," in *Combinatorial Auctions*, eds. P. Cranton, Y. Shoham, and R. Steinberg (Cambridge, MA: MIT Press, 2006), 17–40.

14. The reasons for this are a little complicated but relate to the fact that even a subset of losing bidders can manipulate the final bid price downward by, as counterintuitive as this may seem, *raising* their bids on some items. This makes it harder to pick up on the fact that collusion is taking place. Since we haven't given any details on how multiunit Vickrey auctions are run, it's hard to provide an intuition of how this perverse result comes about. The interested reader with a technical bent can find an explanation in Ausubel and Milgrom, "The Lovely but Lonely Vickrey Auction."

15. Michael H. Rothkopf, "Thirteen Reasons Why the Vickrey-Clarke-Groves Process Is Not Practical," *Operations Research* 55, no. 2 (2007): 191–197.

16. Interested readers can find more details, presented in a nontechnical manner, in John McMillan's *Reinventing the Bazaar: A Natural History of Markets* (New York: W. W. Norton, 2002).

17. Regular folk also got into the act. In *Wireless Nation: The Frenzied Launch of the Cellular Revolution* (New York: Basic Books, 2002), author James Murray tells the story of truck driver Bob Pelissier, whose number came up in an early cellular license lottery in 1985, giving him the license covering Manchester and Nashua, New Hampshire. According to Murray, Pelissier was hardly alone; he told an interviewer in 2001 that "there were literally hundreds of Bob Pelissiers, and we could have told a similar story with different names and a different twist a dozen times at least."

Chapter 6. The Economics of Platforms

1. We thank Pierre Azoulay for encouraging us to look into the Champagne fairs. The sparkling wine that would take its name from the region would not be invented for another 250 years.

2. Quoted in Sheilagh Ogilvie and A. W. Carus, "Institutions and Economic Growth in Historical Perspective," in *The Handbook of Economic Growth*, vol. 2 eds. Philippe Aghion and Steven N. Durlauf (New York: North Holland, 2014), 403–513.

3. These are based on our rough estimates using historical sources.

4. On the fairs, see Sheilagh Ogilvie, *Institutions and European Trade: Merchant Guilds 1000–1800* (New York: Cambridge University Press, 2011), 46; and Jeremy Edwards and Sheilagh Ogilvie, "What Lessons for Economic Development Can We Draw from the Champagne Fairs?" CESifo Working Paper No. 3438, April 2011.

5. Even this is an exaggeration. Every market has some two-sided aspects to it. We haven't looked at the contracts that food producers have with grocery chains, but we'd bet that they lead both parties to care how many boxes of cereal or cans of beans get sold. Even if it's not specified in the contract, you can be sure it'd come up the next time the grocer and its suppliers get together to do business.

6. Jean Tirole and Jean-Charles Rochet convey this point more precisely in a 2006 article where they show that two-sided markets are only necessary when the Coase Theorem fails. This theorem, more a conjecture provided by economist Ronald Coase, essentially argues that free markets maximize efficiency in the absence of externalities or transaction costs. Andrei Hagiu and Julian Wright explore the continuum of reseller and pure marketplace in "Do You Really Want to Be an eBay?" *Harvard Business Review*, March 2013.

7. We thank Pierre Azoulay for this.

8. David S. Evans and Richard Schmalensee, "Markets with Two-Sided Platforms," *Issues in Competition Law and Policy (ABA Section of Antitrust Law)* 1, chap. 28 (2008); Joe Nocera, *A Piece of the Action: How the Middle Class Joined the Moneyed Class* (New York: Simon & Schuster, 1994). Joshua Gans has pointed out that there is some question about whether credit cards are technically platforms.

9. This is distinct from charge cards, which had existed for a while, where you had to pay the full balance at the end of every month.

10. Tirole's work on two-sided markets was done with Jean-Charles Rochet, an economist at the University of Zurich.

11. Paul Samuelson, *Economics* (Cambridge, MA: MIT Press, 1988; first published 1948).

12. Binyamin Appelbaum, "Q. and A. with Jean Tirole, Economics Nobel Winner," The Upshot, *New York Times*, October 14, 2014, www.nytimes.com /2014/10/15/upshot/q-and-a-with-jean-tirole-nobel-prize-winner.html.

13. His precise definition goes somewhat further than this and is framed in terms of whether the level of exchange depends on the prices that participants on different sides of the platform are charged, or just the total price. For example, does it matter whether Visa charges retailers a 3 percent processing fee and offers a 1 percent rebate to cardholders, versus charging a 2 percent processing fee and no rebate? It does (at least when retailers can't

charge a different price for credit card transactions), and hence credit cards qualify as a platform by Tirole's definition.

14. Every feedback system has its imperfections. We know of at least one home renovation victim who claims that his settlement with the contractor stipulated that he refrain from posting feedback on Angie's List.

15. In this sense, the study of platform markets has its roots in the economics of networks, a field that was already well developed by the time Tirole wrote his first platforms paper.

16. The reasons for this are many and also may be about to change. Small retailers, for example, may not even realize they could provide cash discounts. And until recently, card companies forced merchants to treat any card transaction the same. That meant no discount for debit cards, or for lower-cost credit cards relative to higher-cost ones. These constraints are slowly coming undone as a result of legislative and legal actions. The Financial Reform Act of 2010 gave merchants the freedom to set a different card surcharge for, say, debit relative to credit. These changes have been reinforced by litigation from the US Department of Justice. A 2015 court ruling found that the restraints that Amex put on merchants' fees—to be uniform regardless of the credit card fee charged—were in violation of the Sherman Antitrust Act. A number of other countries, for example Australia and the United Kingdom, have already taken steps to crack down on card companies' surcharge rules.

17. Benjamin G. Edelman and Julian Wright, "Price Coherence and Excessive Intermediation," Harvard Business School NOM Unit Working Paper 15–030 (2014).

18. Greg Bensinger, "Competing with Amazon on Amazon," *Wall Street Journal*, June 27, 2012, http://www.wsj.com/articles/SB1000142405270230 4441404577482902055882264.

19. For more on the continuum between pure reseller and pure platform, see the work of Andrei Hagiu.

Chapter 7. Markets Without Prices

1. This is all assuming, of course, that no one in the school gym is interested in a same-sex match, which would complicate matters considerably.

2. David Gales and Lloyd S. Shapley, "College Admissions and the Stability of Marriage," *The American Mathematical Monthly* 69, no. 1 (January 1962): 9–15.

3. See Shapley's biography at the Nobel Prize website: http://www.nobel prize.org/nobel_prizes/economic-sciences/laureates/2012/shapley-bio.html.

4. Alvin E. Roth, *Who Gets What—and Why* (New York: Houghton Mifflin Harcourt, 2015).

5. Personal communication.

6. Gareth Cook, "School Assignment Flaws Detailed: Two Economists Study Problem, Offer Relief," *Boston Globe*, September 12, 2003, https://www2 .bc.edu/~sonmezt/Bostonglobestoryonschoolchoice.htm.

7. Quoted in Nir Vulkan, Alvin E. Roth, and Zvika Neeman, eds., *The Handbook of Market Design* (New York: Oxford University Press, 2013), 145.

8. You can access the series here: http://www.boston.com/news/education /specials/school_chance/articles/.

Chapter 8. Letting Markets Work

1. Viviana Zelizer, *Morals and Markets: The Development of Life Insurance in the United States* (New York: Transaction Publishers, 1983).

2. Marika van Laan, "Art Cache Proves There's Life in Business School, After All," *Chicago Maroon*, April 30, 2013, http://chicagomaroon .com/2013/04/30/art-cache-proves-theres-life-in-business-school-after-all/.

3. These data are from the US Department of Health and Human Services's Organ and Procurement and Transplantation Network.

4. Gary Becker and Julio Elias, "Cash for Kidneys: The Case for a Market for Organs," *Wall Street Journal*, January 18, 2014, http://www.wsj.com /articles/SB10001424052702304149404579322560004817176.

5. Alvin E. Roth, Tayfun Sönmez, and M. Utku Ünver, "Kidney Exchange," *The Quarterly Journal of Economics* (2004): 457–488.

6. The near-simultaneous transfer of four kidneys was completed in 2015 at the University of Kentucky over two grueling days of surgery, though the transfer began with an altruistic donor.

7. "Let Them Eat Pollution," *The Economist*, February 8, 1992, 82.

8. "Summers memo," *Wikipedia*, www.wikipedia.com/wiki/summers_memo.

9. Lydia Polgreen and Marlise Simons, "Global Sludge Ends in Tragedy for Ivory Coast," *New York Times*, October 2, 2006, http://www.nytimes .com/2006/10/02/world/africa/02ivory.html?pagewanted=print&_r=0.

10. William Spain, "Yes, in My Backyard: Tiny Sauget, Illinois Likes Business Misfits," *Wall Street Journal*, October 3, 2006, A1.

11. Recent research has highlighted another problem with platform businesses: if consumers discriminate against minority sellers, then the platform will too. The study finds that "non-black [Airbnb] hosts are able to charge approximately 12% more than black hosts, holding location, rental characteristics, and quality constant." See Benjamin G. Edelman and Michael Luca, "Digital Discrimination: The Case of Airbnb.com," Harvard Business School NOM Unit Working Paper 14-054 (2014). Discrimination may feed into users' feedback, which would, perhaps less directly, lead to discrimination. Although we know of no research on the topic, the concern has seen much attention in the media. See, for example, "The Sharing Economy Is Not as Open as You Might Think," *The Guardian*, November 12, 2014. A post titled "Can the Sharing Economy End Discrimination?" on the website of tech magazine *Wired* took the opposite view, albeit without providing any evidence in support of the argument. For a broader critique of the sharing economy, see Tom Slee, *What's Yours Is Mine* (London: OR Books, 2015).

12. Peter Thiel, "Competition Is for Losers," *Wall Street Journal*, September 12, 2014, http://www.wsj.com/articles/peter-thiel-competition-is-for-losers-1410535536.

Chapter 9. How Markets Shape Us

1. Despite its fearsome reputation, Changi was among the better-run Japanese camps, with only 850 deaths among the 87,000 prisoners who passed through.

2. On Changi as heaven compared to other camps: Kevin Blackburn, "Commemorating and Commodifying the Prisoner of War Experience in South-east Asia: The Creation of Changi Prison Museum," *Journal of the Australian War Memorial* 33 (2000), http://www.awm.gov.au/journal/j33/blackburn.asp.

3. Lee D. Ross, Teresa M. Amabile, and Julia L. Steinmetz, "Social Roles, Social Control, and Biases in Social-Perception Processes," *Journal of Personality and Social Psychology* 35, no. 7 (1977): 485.

4. Nobel laureate Eugene Fama, in work with longtime collaborator Kenneth French, showed in a 2009 study that the vast majority of mutual fund managers do no better than they would have by throwing darts at a dartboard. Yet investors chase after fund managers whose stocks did well the previous year, indicating they believe that the high returns were the result of skill rather than luck.

5. Emily Pronin, Thomas Gilovich, and Lee Ross, "Objectivity in the Eye of the Beholder: Divergent Perceptions of Bias in Self versus Others," *Psychological Review* 111, no. 3 (2004): 781.

6. The experiment was run with subjects drawn from the Israeli Defense Forces. For Hebrew-speaking subjects, the labels were the Bursa and Kommuna Games.

7. Andrei Shleifer, "Does Competition Destroy Ethical Behavior?" *The American Economic Review* 94, no. 2 (2004): 414.

INDEX

Ray Fisman is the Slater Chair in Behavioral Economics at Boston University. Previously, he was Lambert Family Professor of Social Enterprise and codirector of the Social Enterprise Program at the Columbia Business School. He is the author of *The Org*, with Tim Sullivan, and *Economic Gangsters*, with Ted Miguel.

Tim Sullivan is the editorial director of Harvard Business Review Press and has worked at Basic Books, Portfolio, and Princeton University Press, where he helped build one of the most successful academic economics lists in the world.

PublicAffairs is a publishing house founded in 1997. It is a tribute to the standards, values, and flair of three persons who have served as mentors to countless reporters, writers, editors, and book people of all kinds, including me.

I. F. STONE, proprietor of *I. F. Stone's Weekly*, combined a commitment to the First Amendment with entrepreneurial zeal and reporting skill and became one of the great independent journalists in American history. At the age of eighty, Izzy published *The Trial of Socrates*, which was a national bestseller. He wrote the book after he taught himself ancient Greek.

BENJAMIN C. BRADLEE was for nearly thirty years the charismatic editorial leader of *The Washington Post*. It was Ben who gave the *Post* the range and courage to pursue such historic issues as Watergate. He supported his reporters with a tenacity that made them fearless and it is no accident that so many became authors of influential, best-selling books.

ROBERT L. BERNSTEIN, the chief executive of Random House for more than a quarter century, guided one of the nation's premier publishing houses. Bob was personally responsible for many books of political dissent and argument that challenged tyranny around the globe. He is also the founder and longtime chair of Human Rights Watch, one of the most respected human rights organizations in the world.

·   ·   ·

For fifty years, the banner of Public Affairs Press was carried by its owner Morris B. Schnapper, who published Gandhi, Nasser, Toynbee, Truman, and about 1,500 other authors. In 1983, Schnapper was described by *The Washington Post* as "a redoubtable gadfly." His legacy will endure in the books to come.

Peter Osnos, *Founder and Editor-at-Large*